Lessons
from the
Land of the
Bible

Lessons from the Land of the Bible

Clarence H. Wagner, Jr.

Published by Bridges for Peace
Jerusalem, Israel

Printed by Faith Publishing

This book is dedicated to my wife, Pat,
and my two daughters, Ashley and Allison,
who have supported and sojourned with me in the Land of Israel,
as I have pursued God's calling
to reunite the Church
with God's destiny for Israel and the Jewish people.

Acknowledgements

First and foremost, I want to acknowledge the Lord God of Israel who set forth His plan to redeem the world to Himself, showing His love to Israel and His Church, and calling me to be a small part of His divine plan.

I want to thank those who have assisted in the editing and production of this book, giving their skills and providing support to make it possible: Becky Brimmer, Ron Cantrell, Martha Farmer, and Eddelene Marais.

I want to thank those who have inspired me to pursue my calling and shared their insights and encouragement with me over the years: Dr. M. Bernard Resnikoff, Dr. James Fleming, Dr. Marvin Wilson, Jim Monson, Nina Tronstein, JoAnn Magnuson, Ann Thrasher, and my parents, Ann and Clarence Wagner.

I want to thank Oral Roberts, who was used of the Lord when he sent me to Israel in 1977 as the administrator of the Spafford Children's Center. This was part of God's call on my path as the International Director of Bridges for Peace.

Finally, I want to thank the late Dr. G. Douglas Young, the founder of Bridges for Peace, and his wife, Georgina, whose vision became the foundation for all the work and outreach that has been developed over the years.

Clarence H. Wagner, Jr.

Contents

INTRODUCTION
REUNITING THE CHURCH AND ISRAEL

In Matthew 5:17-18, Jesus said, *"Think not that I have come to destroy the Law and the prophets. I came not to destroy them, but to fulfill them."* If Jesus upheld the Law and the prophets, fulfilling the Word of God to the letter, how are we to know Him fully if we only read half a Bible? A New Testament Christian without the Old Testament is like a boat without a rudder. It loses direction and cannot stay on course.

The Gospel of John tells us that Jesus is the Word of God made flesh who came to dwell among us, to be our example, and give us a new life. Therefore, for us to understand God's eternal plan more fully and become better disciples of Jesus, we need to read the whole Bible together as a unit: the Old and New Testaments as one book. In fact, it is more correct to refer to these books as the Older and Newer Testaments of the Bible, so as not to imply that one is somehow better than the other.

If you open most any Bible, you will find a blank page separating the two testaments. A friend of mine, who is a seminary professor, has the annual "tearing of the page" on his first day in class with his new students. They all locate this one dividing page and tear it out of their Bibles to symbolically reconnect the two testaments as one Book.

We all need to do this, not only physically, but spiritually. We need to reconnect with the whole of God's Word, appreciating that the Old Testament is the New Testament concealed and the New Testament is the Old Testament revealed. Neither has the complete picture, as both together give us God's complete revelation.

For the past 2,000 years, the Church has, for the most part, worked to separate itself from its Jewish roots. This is a violation of Paul's clear message that we are wild branches grafted into the olive tree (Rom. 11:13-24). The olive tree represents God's covenants and promises made to Israel, which we became a part of when we received our salvation (Eph. 2:12-13). Paul warned us against separating and becoming arrogant (Rom. 11:20), knowing that the root holds up the branches, not the other way around. Sadly, the Church's rejection of its Jewish roots has led to heresies in the Church, the integration of pagan practices, and the persecution of the Jewish people by the Church throughout the centuries.

However, this is beginning to change. Today, a small ray of light is beginning to shine in both the Church and Israel. Both are rediscovering each other and a new dynamic is taking place. As God is restoring His land and people, Israel, in fulfillment of Bible prophecy and in preparation for the soon coming of Messiah, Christians are rediscovering their Jewish roots, while Jews are meeting Christians who truly love and pray for them and the nation of Israel. In the past, Christians persecuted Jews in the name of Jesus. Today, because of Jesus, *"the dividing wall of hostility"* is coming down, just as He had planned from the beginning (Eph. 2:14-18).

Lessons from the Land of the Bible is a collection of lessons which

11

was originally presented on our television program, *Jerusalem Mosaic*. Unable to give the fullest teaching in only a few minutes on TV, each chapter expands the lessons for more careful study and understanding. They are divided into three categories - *The Hebraic Roots of the New Testament, The Land of Israel and Prophecy,* and *Christian-Jewish Understanding.* Each lesson draws us closer to God's heart to reunite the Church and Israel, helping us to better understand God's Word and His plan for the world, while making us better disciples of Jesus.

I hope these lessons will whet your appetite to learn more, so that you will contact your nearest national office of Bridges for Peace. Get on our mailing list to receive my monthly *Israel Teaching Letter* and other study materials so that you can continue to learn. Our *Jerusalem Mosaic* program is also available as an educational video series you won't want to miss. (See page 184 for more information).

May the Lord God of Israel be glorified in this work, which is but a taste of so much more the Lord wants to teach us.

Clarence H. Wagner, Jr.
Host - *Jerusalem Mosaic*
International Director - Bridges for Peace
Jerusalem

Part I

The Hebraic Roots
of the
New Testament

*Yeshua (Jesus) said, "Think not that I
have come to destroy the law and the prophets.
I came not to destroy them, but to fulfill them"
(Matthew 5:17-18).*

The Hebraic Roots of the New Testament

The New Testament was written in a type of scriptural shorthand. The writers assumed that we already understood the depth and meaning of the Old Testament, the Hebrew language in which it was written, the culture, and the religious practices of the biblical period.

Examples used to explain the character and nature of God, how He relates to man, and us to Him, were expressed in common symbols understood by everyone of their day.

However, 2,000 years later and thousands of miles from Israel where the Bible was written, we often miss the richness of the New Testament teachings. This is because we have lost our understanding of these symbols, the language and cultural background.

Another problem for those of us in western nations is that we think with a very Greek mindset, while the writers of the Bible were Hebrew-minded. Sixty-four of the sixty-six books of the Bible were written by Jewish writers as they were inspired by God. Their style was uniquely different than how we have been taught to think by our western educational systems. Therefore, we often miss the unwritten messages "between the lines."

What do I mean by being Greek-minded or Hebrew-minded?

The Greek mind is more interested in form and structure, while the Hebrew mind is more interested in the function. In other words, the Greek mind is always looking at things analytically, asking, "What is it?" On the other hand, the Hebrew mind is more interested in asking, "What does it do?"

To illustrate what I mean, let's consider a plastic bottle of spring water.

If I held one up and asked you to describe it, many of you would tell me that it is about 8 inches high, made of plastic, is corrugated, has a cap, and is clear. That is how the Greeks thought, who were more interested in defining the form of an object. The Hebrew mind, which is more interested in the function, would describe this water bottle as a container: it can hold liquids, you could use it as a vase, you could put colored water in it and use it for decoration, if you had two of them - you could make really gaudy earrings. (Smile!)

I think you get my point. The Hebrew mind was more interested in what you could DO with an object, not on how it was constructed.

Therefore, we need to read our Bibles with a Hebrew mindset, knowing that if we understand the function of an object or concept used in the Bible, it will tell us more about the character of God or our relationship to Him.

The lessons in this section take a fresh look at some well-known New Testament events or symbols. Researching them, I realized that there was so much unsaid "between the lines." Then, I became very excited when the messages revealed so much more about my relationship to

Jesus and the Father, Who love us and want to bless us in so many ways.

Who doesn't want to be a better disciple of the Lord? Yet, how can we, if we are only getting part of the message from our Bibles due to translation errors and our lack of knowledge about our Old Testament, Hebraic roots? These messages will show you the richness of God's Word and hopefully inspire you to keep on digging yourself. We are called to *"study to show ourselves approved"* (II Tim. 2:15).

Our ministry, Bridges for Peace, has many resources to help you. Please see our resource section at the end of the book to make contact with us. We will help you continue to learn many more lessons from the land of the Bible.

LESSONS FROM THE OLIVE TREE

Chapter 1

Trees are such a precious gift from the Lord. They not only provide oxygen for us to breathe, but also food to eat, wood for building houses and furniture, pulp for paper, fuel for warmth, and shade for rest and recreation. In their great variety, trees provide natural beauty for our eyes to behold.

Some species of trees are known for their special qualities. The "mighty" oak is known for its durability and strength. The "whispering" pine provides a soft hush in the background as the wind blows through its needles. The weeping willow displays its cascading branches that gracefully sway in the breeze, often overhanging a quiet pond.

IMPORTANCE OF THE OLIVE TREE

One of the most remarkable trees is the olive tree. Most of us are not too familiar with olive trees because they don't grow near where we live. However, in the land of the Bible, it was, and is, the most important of all the trees because it is a source of food, light, hygiene and healing.

When I first came to Israel, I was fascinated by the olive trees which are found covering the terraced mountainsides in the Galilee, Judea and Samaria. They are beautiful to look at with their unique gnarled and twisted trunks and evergreen tops. Just looking at them you have a sense that they have a grace and character that sets them apart from other trees. As with other common symbols in Israel, the characteristics of the olive tree are used by the writers of the Bible to tell us more about God, about Israel, and our relationship to both.

17

Olive trees, their fruit, and the oil of their fruit have long played an important role in the daily life of Israel. For nearly 8,000 years, olives have been eaten as a Mediterranean staple food and olive oil has been used for cooking, in lamps for light (Ex. 27:20, Lev. 24:2), for medicine, and for anointing oil in religious ceremonies (Ex. 30:24-25). By the time of the Roman conquest of Judea, the olive had become one of the most basic dietary items, even of the poor.

The trees were always plentiful around the countryside and are known for their tenacity. They grow in almost any condition: on terraced hills or in valleys, in rocky or fertile soil. They can thrive in great heat with a minimum of water, and are virtually indestructible. Some grow from root systems 2,000 years old, yet the olive producer has to wait fifteen years for his first good harvest. It was an olive leaf that a dove from Noah's ark brought to Noah, *"Then the dove came to him in the evening, and behold, a freshly plucked olive leaf was in her mouth; and Noah knew that the waters had receded from the earth"* (Gen. 8:11). Whatever else succumbed to the flood waters, the hearty olive tree was still alive. At least since the time of Julius Caesar, one of the universal emblems of peace has been that of the olive branch.

Olive oil was so plentiful in Israel that it was one of the products regularly exported. Solomon sent the King of Tyre 100,000 gallons (378,533 liters) of olive oil (I Kgs. 5:11). One thousand years later, during the time of Yeshua (Jesus), olive oil is mentioned in writings of that day as the only export of the Jerusalem region. The Mount of Olives, located just east of the Old City of Jerusalem, attests to the prevalence of olive trees around the city. Also, it was in the Garden of Gethsemane (*Gat Shemen* in Hebrew, literally, the place of the "olive press"), where Yeshua spent much of His time in

Jerusalem with His disciples. *"Coming out, He went to the Mount of Olives, as He was accustomed, and His disciples also followed Him"* (Lk. 22:39).

LESSONS FROM THE PSALMS

Primarily, the olive tree symbolizes faithfulness and steadfastness.

Psalms 52:8 says, *"But I am like a green olive tree in the house of God; I trust in the mercies of God forever and ever."*

No matter what the conditions: hot, dry, cold, wet, rocky, or sandy, the evergreen olive tree will live and produce fruit. It is said that you can never kill an olive tree. Even when cut down or burned, new shoots will emerge from its roots. This Scripture passage reminds us that no matter the conditions of life, we should remain steadfast as the olive tree in the presence of God - evergreen (faithful) and bearing fruit.

Psalms 128:3 says, *"Your wife shall be like a fruitful vine in the very heart of your house; Your children like olive plants all around your table."*

The analogy of your children being *"like olive plants all around your table"* would tell the ancient Bible reader that his offspring would be plentiful, hearty, and even dutifully responsive to the parents. All you have to do is look at almost any olive tree and you will see as many as ten or more new tree shoots growing up out of the root system around the tree. Psalms 128:3 would have been a comforting and faithful promise from the Lord!

THE OLIVE TREE, ISRAEL AND THE CHURCH

The most striking use of the image of the olive tree in the Bible is in Romans 11 where Paul describes the relationship between Israel (the Jewish people and God's ancient and ongoing covenantal relationship) and the Church. In fact, the entire three chapters of Romans 9-11 are focused on this topic and culminate with the olive tree image. (PLEASE take time to read this passage.) Paul shows us that the olive tree represents the covenants and promises to Israel, growing from its holy Root, which is the Messiah, the Word of God. The natural branches are the people of Israel. Those who turned away from that relationship were broken off.

Christians are simply the wild branches grafted in among the natural branches to *"became a partaker with them of the root and fatness of the olive tree,"* which God established (Rom. 11:17).

It is evident from Scripture, as well as from nature, that the root and trunk support the branches, and not vice versa (11:18). In this position, there is no room for pride or the notion that we Christians have replaced Israel (the Jewish people), or that God rejected His own covenants and promises in the Hebrew Scriptures (the Old Testament). There is no room for boasting and arrogance, as the Church has been prone to do, as both the natural branches and the engrafted wild branches only remain by faith (Rom. 11:18-21). The Church is an extention of a plan that pre-existed it. Therefore, there should only be Godly fear (11:20) and thankfulness for the Lord's great mercies to us (11:33-36), as well as an attitude of love and mercy towards the Jewish people who are beloved for the sakes of the fathers (Rom. 11:28). After all, it is through Israel and His covenant people that God gave us everything we Christians hold spiritually dear! There is only one tree, not two, and we "wild branches" have been privileged to drink in new life from the cultivated, established tree.

Historically, the Church has not honored these passages as it not only boasted against the Jewish people (the natural branches), but severely persecuted them to the point of death.

Often, the Church has lacked even the most basic understanding of our Hebrew roots. Also, it has not recognized that we cannot fully grasp who we are, without acknowledging these roots.

As a result, the historical Church has sadly perpetrated outrageous acts towards the "natural branches" (the Jewish people) during the Crusades, the Inquisition, the Pogroms, and even in the formulations of the teachings that became a religious justification for Hitler's Final Solution of the so-called "Jewish problem" in the Holocaust. Instead of mercy, Christianity showed contempt.

HONORING OUR ROOTS

The prophet Isaiah said, *"Look to the rock from which you were cut and to the quarry from which you were hewn; look to Abraham, your father, and to Sarah, who gave you birth"* (Isa. 51:1-2).

Christianity did not spring forth from a vacuum. It sprang from the highly developed religious tradition and culture of ancient Israel. It is all too easy for us Gentiles to forget this all-important fact.

For instance, if Yeshua were presented to us today, His "Jewishness" would probably shock most Christians. Yet, we know from Scripture that a woman once came to Him and touched the *tzit-tzit*, or fringes, of His garment (Luke 8:44). He wore the garments of Jewish tradition, just as many orthodox Jews do today, fulfilling the commands of the Law (Dt. 22:12).

Likewise, the earliest church was a Jewish church. It was headquartered in the Jewish capital, Jerusalem, and was presided over by a Jewish leader.

Yeshua said, *"Think not that I came to destroy the Law and the prophets...I came not to destroy them but to fulfill them!"* (Mt. 5:17-18). God is *"the same yesterday, today, and forever"* (Heb. 13:8). As Christians, we should see that Yeshua epitomized the Law and the teachings of the prophets as the living Word of God. And yet, so many of us know so little of the Tanach, the Hebrew Scriptures.

Christians refer to these writings of the "Old Testament" as though the term "old" means it is of little value when compared with the "new." Yet, without the "old," the "new" loses much of its meaning, and it is often misinterpreted or not fully interpreted. When we do this, we are missing out on much God has for us in His Word.

It was from this "Jewish/Hebrew" perspective that the Church began to reach out to the world of the Gentiles. It was as if Judaism had been uniquely tailored by Yeshua and the apostles to be made "attractive" to Gentiles. Gentiles would now be able to receive the Jewish Scriptures, to heed the Jewish prophets, and to sing the Jewish Psalms. As Paul went out with the Gospel message, he was careful to stress that the message was emanating from Jerusalem and Israel. He encouraged Gentile saints to collect funds for the needy in Jerusalem (I Cor. 16:2-4); he referred difficult doctrinal decisions to Jerusalem and to the Jewish elders there (Acts 15:2); his Gospel journeys usually began or ended in Jerusalem. He even gave the Gentile church an example of keeping Jewish feasts in Jerusalem (Acts 20:16).

The Apostle Paul did something else as he ministered among Gentiles. He stressed the importance of keeping the right attitude toward Israel and the Jewish people. That attitude was to be one of humility (Rom. 11:20), mercy (Rom. 11:31) and kindness, even to the point of stressing an obligation in sharing material gifts with the people of Israel (Rom. 15:27). It was a wonderful ideal. But, in time, Paul's exhortations began to go unheeded.

There were many factors which brought about the vast chasm which exists today between Israel and the Church. The two unsuccessful wars fought by the Jews against the Romans in AD 70 and in AD 133-135 undoubtedly did much to strain relations, since the early Church refused to help their Jewish brothers in these wars. Instead, in AD 70, the Church fled to Pella, across the Jordan River, following the warning of Matthew 24:16, believing the end of the world was at hand.

The very vulnerability and isolation of the early Church also might have contributed to their sense of separation from those who began to persecute them.

Finally, the early Church Fathers certainly did not help the situation, since many were openly anti-Semitic. The young Church fought for its life against Roman persecution from without and heresies from within. All this led the Church toward exclusivism and into taking a stand against its Jewish roots.

With the conversion of Emperor Constantine in the early fourth century, and the subsequent "Christianization" of the whole Roman Empire, this anti-Semitic trend became crystallized. The Church moved rapidly to rid itself of all Jewish trappings. For example, the Christian holiday of Easter was divorced from its Jewish origins in the Passover; Saturday (Sabbath), the biblically prescribed day of rest and worship, was changed to Sunday; Pentecost was disassociated from Shavuot, etc., as the Church attempted to cast off the influence of "this odious people" (as the Jews were described by some Church leaders).

A theology generally termed as Triumphalism began to be in vogue. The same theology has persisted to this day, occasionally finding renewal under different names, including Replacement Theology.

Basically, this belief proclaims that God is finished with the Jews: that Christianity has indeed replaced Judaism and that the Church is the true Israel. This theology universally applies all the scriptural blessings to the Church, and all the curses to Israel.

To show the fallacy of this teaching, read Romans 9-11 and everywhere it reads "Israel," replace it with the words, "the Church." You will quickly see how erroneous is this theology. Israel is Israel, even in the New Testament. And, when the Gentile Church is included in that concept, we are given that position by virtue of "grafting in," "adoption," "partakers," and being "made near:" never by "replacing."

Of course, the almost immediate result of such a theology was the outright persecution of Israel by the Church. This malady has persisted through most of the 2,000 years of Christian history, contributing even to the Nazi Holocaust. It is surprising for most Christians to learn that Hitler only put into practice what the Church in Europe had believed and taught for centuries. (See chapter 14)

Even today, after this awful disaster, anti-Semitism abounds in the Church. An example of this is seen in the fact that many otherwise loving Christians are suspicious of "those Jews."

I see many pastors and parishioners who are happy to visit Israel and see where Jesus walked, but they have utterly no interest in the miraculous and prophetic renewal of the Jewish state, which is now in progress. Perhaps this is an expression of the ultimate in anti-Semitism, the denial that the Jewish people have any place in God's plan today.

RECOVERING OUR ROOTS

What we see prescribed in the Bible is a far cry from what we see in the Church today. We see that God had purposed from the outset that Gentiles are to be a part of His plan, but not the whole plan. We receive glimpses of this program of God as far back as Father Abraham. God promised the patriarch Abraham that he would be the father of multitudes of *goyim* (peoples, nations, Gentiles) (Gen. 17:4), and that all nations would be blessed in him (Gen. 12:3). This theme is carried on in the descendants of Abraham. We see it particularly in Joseph, who was married to a Gentile woman in Egypt.

One of his children, Ephraim, was destined to become one of the most numerous and powerful tribes in the Northern Kingdom. The blessing upon the head of this little Jewish lad was this, that he would be the father of multitudes of Gentiles (Gen. 48:19). Much later, Ephraim was dispersed into the nations, along with the other nine "lost tribes." The dispersion of these Jews among the nations, their effect upon nations, and their recovery and restoration to their land, still remains a mystery too great for us to fathom.

We see the theme picked up again in the woman Rahab, who was saved from the doomed city of Jericho and allowed to join with the people of Israel; and again as the prophet Isaiah describes the Messiah of Israel, called the "Root of Jesse." It is said that this Messiah would *"stand as a*

banner for the peoples (Gentiles); the nations will rally to him, and his place of rest will be glorious" (Isa. 11:10). But perhaps we see the theme of Gentiles being joined to Israel most clearly in Ruth the Moabitess, who was not only allowed access into Israel, but who became the great-grandmother of King David.

The beautiful story of Ruth expresses for us most clearly what a proper attitude toward Israel should be. In fact, this woman seems to illustrate, in her life, most of the fruits of the Spirit mentioned by Paul in Galatians 5:22-23. She was truly devoted to her Israelite mother-in-law. She loved her with a deep love and commitment which led her to forsake her own heritage, and even her country, in order to be with Naomi. When Ruth arrived in Israel it was not with a feeling of superiority as many Christians have today. Instead, *"she bowed down with her face to the ground..."* (Ruth 2:10). She was willing to abase herself to a position lower than a servant girl's (2:13). Her attitude was one of continual mercy and generosity as she shared her meager gleanings with Naomi (2:18).

The life of Ruth was also marked with obedience (3:5), kindness (3:10), holiness (3:10), discretion (3:14), true love, faithfulness and commitment to Israel (4:15). Ruth said to Naomi, *"Where you go I will go, and where you stay I will stay. Your people will be my people and your God my God"* (Ruth 1:16).

Perhaps in Ruth's life we get a visual example of what the engrafting into the olive tree of Romans 11 is all about. It is time that we, the Church, put aside our arrogance and, in humility, understand what it means to be that wild olive branch graciously grafted in by God to receive from Israel those everlasting covenants, promises and hopes that we have been "made near" (Eph. 2:11-13) -- lest we be broken off for our arrogance and boasting.

Let us honor our roots and show love and mercy to God's natural branches!

THE HEM OF THE GARMENT

Chapter 2

Despite the development in the Land of Israel since the founding of the State of Israel, you can still walk along the shores of the Sea of Galilee and imagine what it was like when Yeshua (Jesus) was ministering there. He was almost always followed by throngs of people eager to hear His teaching. It was along the sea that a very sick woman caught up with Him, desperate to be healed of a chronic ailment. This miracle story is very well-known to readers of the New Testament. Yet, there is so much that is "between the lines" which, when understood, will strengthen your relationship with the Lord. This involves tassels, snails, authority, humility, and wings. I know you are thinking, "What is this all about?" Read on!

TASSELS

In Matthew 9:20-22, we find a curious story of a sick woman receiving healing simply by touching Jesus' clothes: *"Just then a woman, who had been subject to bleeding for twelve years, came up behind Him and touched the hem of His garment; for she said to herself, 'If I only touch His cloak, I will be healed.' Jesus (Yeshua) turned and saw her. 'Take heart, daughter,' He said, 'your faith has healed you.' And the woman was healed from that moment."*

In the Mark account of the same story, it continues:

"At once Yeshua realized that power had gone out from Him. He turned around in the crowd and asked, 'Who touched My clothes?' 'You see the people crowding against You,' His disciples answered, 'and yet You can ask, Who touched Me?'" (Mk. 5:30-31).

What is so significant about the hem of Jesus' garment? At first reading, it seems an odd practice. However, once we understand the significance of the hem of one's garment,

25

these passages will have much more meaning.

The word translated, hem, is actually referring to the fringes, or tassels (called *tzitziyot*, in Hebrew), required to be on the four corners of all clothing of Jewish men, in accordance with God's instruction:

"The Lord said to Moses, 'Speak to the Israelites and say to them: Throughout the generations to come, you are to make tassels on the corners of one's garments, with a blue cord on each tassel. You will have these tassels to look at and so will remember all the commands of the Lord, that you may obey them and not prostitute yourselves by going after the lusts of your own hearts and eyes. Then you will remember to obey all My commands, and will be consecrated to your God. I am the Lord your God.'"(Num. 15:37-41a)

In ancient Israel, men wore four-cornered outer tunics with these tassels, or *tzitziyot*, tied to the four corners. This outer garment became known as a *tallit*, and eventually evolved into the more formal *prayer shawl*.

But, why tassels? These tassels were to remind each Jewish man of his responsibility to fulfill God's commandments. In fact, these tassels are

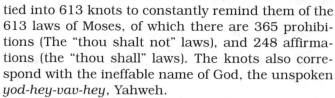

tied into 613 knots to constantly remind them of the 613 laws of Moses, of which there are 365 prohibitions (The "thou shalt not" laws), and 248 affirmations (the "thou shall" laws). The knots also correspond with the ineffable name of God, the unspoken *yod-hey-vav-hey*, Yahweh.

Because they were hanging on the four corners of your garment, in full view of everyone including yourself, they would be a constant reminder to walk according to God's Laws. The Hebrew word we translate as Law, is *halacha*, and it literally means "walk." You see, following God's law is a daily walk, and to stay on His path of righteousness, we all need constant reminding.

Wearing these tassels would be comparable to us wearing a large Bible on a rope around our necks. How would we behave in public, how would we speak to others, where would be go? God intended them to be a constant reminder of His Word when he told the Israelites to wear these fringes.

Today, because Jewish people wear western clothes, they keep this law by wearing a four-cornered garment as an undershirt. Yet, they bring the tassels out over their belt so that they can be seen. We also find the *tzitziyot* on the corners of the beautiful prayer shawls worn by Jewish men as an outer garment when they pray. I always like to see the men in my neighborhood in Jerusalem coming home from synagogue every Friday night and Saturday morning with their flowing prayer shawls draped over their shoulders.

When deep in prayer, Jewish men will put these prayer shawls over their heads to shut out the world and be in the presence of God. This can be seen in the synagogue or at the Western Wall in Jerusalem. The prayer shawls are white, representing the heavens, or the dwelling place of the Lord. And, the color blue represents the *Ruach HaKodesh*, or Holy Spirit of God. Therefore, praying under the *tallit*, or prayer shawl, is covering yourself with the presence of God. From biblical times, this custom was like a prayer closet, and it is likely this is what Yeshua was referring to in Matthew 6:6, when He told us to get into our closet, apart from the people around, and pray in secret to the Lord.

This *tallit* was the mantle worn by Samuel (I Sam. 15:27), and it was Elijah's mantle that was conferred upon Elisha (I Kgs. 19:19). It was also worn by Yeshua, and

The prayer shawl is used as a prayer closet.

the "hem of the garment" that was touched by the woman with the issue of blood was actually the *tzitziyot* or tassels of His *tallit*.

Even in His glorious Second Coming, Yeshua will be wearing His *tallit*. In Revelation 19:11-16, John gives us a description: *"I saw heaven standing open and there before me was a white horse, whose rider is Faithful and True, ... He has a name written on Him that no one but He Himself knows. He is clothed in a garment dipped in blood: and His Name is The Word of God... On His garment and on His thigh He has a name written: King of Kings, and Lord of Lords"* (Rev. 19:11-13,16). J. R. Church suggests that the vesture is the *tallit* of Yeshua with His titles written upon it and on His thighs. Where do the *tzitziyot* fall, but on one's thigh? Notice there are four titles listed in this passage - perhaps one for each of the four *tzitziyot*:

1. *"A Name written, that no man knew but He Himself"* - the ineffable name of God, Yahweh! (v. 12)
2. *"The Word of God"* (v. 13)
3. *"King of Kings"* and,
4. *"Lord of Lords"* (v. 16).

The purpose of the four fringes on a garment was, and is, and still will be to proclaim the Word of the Lord, so as to remember them and perform them.

SNAILS

Each tassel was to have a blue thread. With blue so prevalent in our world today, it is hard to imagine that during the entire biblical period, blue was probably the most expensive color to produce. Therefore, it was reserved for royalty and the wealthy who could afford it.

Before synthetic dyes, the only source was a small gland in the murex snail. It took 12,000 snails to fill up a thimble of blue dye. In 200 BC, one pound of cloth, dyed blue, cost the equivalent of $36,000. By AD 300, this same pound of blue cloth cost $96,000. This indicates that Lydia, the seller of purple and an early convert of Christianity, was one of the wealthiest women in the Empire (Acts 16:14).

In the "shorthand" of the Bible, this tidbit of information about Lydia, which means very little to us today, said a lot to early readers of the text. It said, in effect, "Hey, one of the wealthiest and most influential people in the Roman Empire has gotten saved!" Imagine the impact this would make on the message of the Gospel.

Blue also represented something divine, which is why royal blue set people apart from the rest of the common world. Therefore, to have a blue thread was to have something of the divine and royal, and served to remind each wearer of his significance in God's sight. After all, God calls us to be a royal priesthood.

This treasured thread would probably have been passed on from a father to his son as one of his precious legacies. The blue stripe on the prayer shawl of Jewish men has the same meaning, and interestingly, this symbol is represented in the blue stripes on the flag of Israel today.

The flag of Israel, much maligned in the world, is really a representation of the Lord in all its elements. The white background and blue stripes come from the prayer shawl. The Star of David in the middle has been given a number of explanations. One I like is from the Jewish scholar, Franz Rosensweig, who interprets it this way. The Star of David is made up of two triangles. One is the representation of God as He is manifested as Creator, Redeemer and Teacher. Sound familiar? The other triangle represents God, man and others in a three-way relationship that requires all three elements to manifest the working out of God's Word in our lives. To me, this makes the Israeli flag a true standard and representation of God, and a testimony to the Israeli people of whom they serve and why they exist. Spiritually speaking, perhaps this is why the flag of Israel, like the people and state of Israel, gets so much opposition in the secular world we live in today.

AUTHORITY

These tassels also came to be associated with a person's authority.

Saul and David: In the case of King Saul, we find that David humiliated him by sneaking up to him in a cave at the Spring of Ein Gedi and cutting off Saul's tassels, a symbol of his authority.

David's men said:

"This is the day the Lord spoke of when He said to you, 'I will give your enemy into your hands for you to deal with as you wish'... Afterward, David was conscience-stricken for having cut off a corner of Saul's robe. He said to his men, 'The Lord forbid that I should do such a thing to my mas-

ter, the Lord's anointed, or lift my hand against him; for he is the anointed of the Lord'" (I Sam. 24:4-6).

Why was David upset with himself? Because he understood that to steal someone's tassel was to steal his authority. Even though David did this to prove to Saul that he was not trying to kill him, the symbol of taking the corner fringe would be humiliation to Saul. This bothered David.

David immediately went out of the cave and prostrated himself in humility before Saul to prove to Saul that he was not trying to kill him. David said:

"Why do you listen when men say, 'David is bent on harming you?' This day have you seen with your own eyes how the Lord delivered you into my hands in the cave. Some urged me to kill you, but I spared you; I said, 'I will not lift my hand against my master, because he is the Lord's anointed.' See, my father, look at this piece of your robe in my hand! I cut off the corner of your robe, but did not kill you. Now understand and recognize that I am not guilty of wrongdoing or rebellion. I have not wronged you, but you are hunting me down to take my life..." (I Sam. 24:8-11).

Everyone, including Saul, knew that David had been anointed by Samuel to be the next king, which is why Saul feared David. At Ein Gedi, David had literally taken Saul's authority and at that point, he probably could have taken the throne from Saul. But, he didn't; rather, he let God choose the time for him to receive the throne. This act convinced Saul that David was telling the truth.

David's act of giving back Saul's authority also reconciled the two men. Saul said:

"May the Lord reward you well for the way you treated me today. I know that you will surely be king and that the kingdom of Israel will be established in your hands" (I Sam. 24:19b-20).

Boaz and Ruth: Another example of the authority represented in the tassel is found in a passage in the book of Ruth, which is sometimes difficult to understand. In Chapter three, Ruth went to Boaz to receive his blessing that would help her out of her difficult situation. She went to the threshing floor and slept at his feet.

"In the middle of the night something startled the man, and he turned and discovered a woman lying at his feet. 'Who are you?' he asked. 'I am your servant, Ruth,' she said. 'Spread the corner of your garment over me, since you are a kinsman redeemer'" (Ruth 3:8-9).

He immediately understood and said to her:

"Don't be afraid. I will do for you all you ask. All my fellow townsmen know that you are a woman of noble character" (Ruth 3:11).

He proceeded to make every arrangement to help her, and eventually, he married her.

What Ruth did in asking Boaz to spread the corner of his garment over her was a symbolic way of saying she was placing herself under Boaz's authority.

HUMILITY

By the end of the Second Temple period (70 BC - AD 135), tassels had become a symbol of social status. The wealthier you were, the more grand your tassels might appear. This is human nature, since we might also be tempted to "show-off" with a public display, e,g. the kind of car we drive, the house we live in, or the jewelry we wear. It is known that during the time of Yeshua, the tassels of some Pharisees were so long and elaborate, that they dragged on the ground. It was this ostentatious display of pride that Yeshua was rebuking when He said, *"They make...the tassels of their prayer shawls long..."* (Mt. 23:5).

In speaking of the Pharisees, it is important to realize that not all Pharisees were hypocrites. Nicodemus was a Pharisee (John 3). They were the conservative religious leaders of the time. In fact, of them Yeshua said, *"[They] sit in Moses' seat. So you must obey them and do everything they tell you. But do not do what they do, for they do not practice what they preach"* (Mt. 23:2-3). Just as in our time, some religious leaders were good and godly people; others were charlatans. Because of the references to some who were all show and no heart, Christians today often mistakenly think all Pharisees were unsavory types. Theologically, Yeshua was much closer to the Pharisees than to the Sadducees.

The lesson for all of us from this passage is that it is more important to perform God's commandments from inward conviction, in humility, than by simply wearing it on the outside with overdone religious practices. God looks upon the heart, while man often looks upon outward appearances (I Sam. 16:7).

UNDER HIS WINGS

Let's go back to the woman on the shores of the Sea of Galilee who came to Jesus for healing.

When she pressed through the crowd, she was not content to just pat Jesus on the back. She was a desperate woman, who had spent all of her money on cures that did not work. It was a bold step for her to push through that crowd of people, for according to Levitical law, it was forbidden for her to be out in public with her condition, for she was considered unclean (Lev. 15:25). However, she was at the end of her rope. She had nothing to lose. She had heard of the Messiah who could heal and she anxiously sought Him out.

But why did she want to touch the hem of His garment - the tassels of His *tallit*?

These *tzitziyot* were a point of contact she needed to help her release her faith to receive a miracle in her life.

What did they represent?

First, they represented the Word of God, which is always the place where we can find healing for all the needs in our life.

Second, the fringes also represented the authority of Yeshua. She had heard that many people were healed by Yeshua, that He taught with authority, and when He spoke, people were healed.

Third, there was even more to these fringes. The prophet Malachi spoke of the Messiah of Israel and said of Him, *"But for you who revere My name, the sun of righteousness will rise with healing in His wings"* (Mal. 4:2).

The Hebrew word for "wings" used in this passage is *kanaf*, which is a word that specifically means the fringe-like feathers or edges of a bird's wing, not the whole wing. All of us have seen an eagle or hawk circling in the summer sky and have seen these fringe-like feathers. This word, therefore, had two meanings and could be translated wings, or fringes.

The woman had heard Yeshua was the Messiah. Perhaps she remembered this messianic promise from the scroll of Malachi and thought, if I am to be healed, then will it be found in His wings... His *tzitziyot*? By faith, she reached out and touched the fringes, and was healed.

It is interesting that all though the Old Testament, the Hebrew word for wings in most passages is *kanaf* when referring to God. Surely, the place of refuge is under the *kanaf* of the Lord, i.e., under His Word and His authority!

In a different passage, some time later Yeshua arrived at the town of Genessaret, also on the shores of the Sea of Galilee. The men of the town recognized Yeshua and sent word out so that many people brought all their sick to Him and begged Him to let the sick just touch the fringe of His garment. The Bible simply reports, *"all who touched Him were healed"* (Mk. 6:53-56).

These people were not healed simply by touching the fringes of Yeshua's garment in a crowd. They were healed when their faith touched the power of God and the One who could heal their infirmities. It was their point of contact to release their faith to receive a touch from the Lord.

What about you and me? None of us is without a need in our life, whether it be healing, family problems, financial or emotional problems. Do we have the simple faith to reach out and touch the hem of the garment of Yeshua? If you do, He is waiting to meet our needs, even today.

This Lesson from the Land of the Bible is found in our
Jerusalem Mosaic Video Series, Program #101,
along with other exciting features.
Please turn to page 186 to order your copy.

WHAT'S IN A NAME?

Chapter 3

In our world, each species or animal has a name, such as the lion, ibex, or ostrich. This is also true for all birds, fish and even plants and insects.

Names are very important, and each of us also has a name.

What's your name?

- Richard, Larry, Ted, Jim?
- Mary, Ann, Donna, Stephanie?

Names have a meaning. Expectant parents pore over books like "10,000 Baby Names," which give meanings and multiple spellings for many names.

In the 20th century, most of us have named our children after someone we admire, or we simply choose a first name that sounds appropriate with the family name. The meaning behind the name is generally given less attention than in ancient times.

For example, we love our daughter Ashley's name. But, its actual meaning from Old English is, "from the ash tree meadow" — not exactly steeped with profound meaning. Our other daughter, Allison, is named after her grandfather. However, her name also means, "truthful,"

Seal bearing the name "Eliashib, son of Ishiahu." Israelite period, found at Kibbutz Ramat Rachel near Jerusalem.

which is certainly an important virtue. In modern Jewish life the naming of a child is still an important occasion. Boys receive their Hebrew names on the eighth day of life, at the circumcision ceremony. A baby girl is named in the synagogue during the first Torah reading following her birth.

THE IMPORTANCE OF NAMES IN THE BIBLE

In ancient Israelite households, the naming of a child carried more importance than in many 20th century Western homes. The ancients were interested in what a name meant, as it expressed a character trait hoped for the child.

33

Sometimes a child received the name of a favorite grandparent. However, most often, parents named their children as a praise to God or a statement of faith, e.g. Elijah, "My God is Adonai;" Isaiah, "God is salvation;" or Jonathan, "God has given."

Others seemed to get names from peculiar sources, e.g. Miriam, meaning "fat, thick or strong;" or after animals, e.g. Jonah, meaning "dove;" or Leah, meaning "wild cow."

Isaiah had a great sense of his prophetic calling. He named his two sons with prophetic names so that when they were called, a prophetic truth was proclaimed. One was named, *Maher-shalal-hash-baz*, (quick to the plunder, swift to the spoil) in reference to the coming destruction of Damascus and Samaria (Isa. 8:1-4). His other son was called, *Shear-Yashuv* (a remnant will return), a reference to Isaiah's longing for the Israelites' return.

Some people and places received their names because of the circumstances prevailing at the time of naming, e.g. Jacob called the place where he wrestled with the Lord, Peniel, *"For I have seen God face to face..."* (Gen. 32:30). Peniel, in Hebrew, literally means, "the face of God." In Bethlehem, as Rachel was dying in childbirth, she named her newborn Ben-Oni (Son of my Sorrow), but Jacob immediately renamed the boy, Benjamin (Son of the Right Hand).

Most ancient peoples did not receive a family name (last name) and a given name, as we do today. However, by the time of the New Testament period, we see people were adding descriptive appendages to help identify a person: 1) where they were from, e.g. Joseph of Arimathea, Paul of Tarsus, Jesus of Nazareth; 2) who was their father, e.g. Jesus bar (son of) Jonah; 3) by their profession, e.g. Simon the Tanner; or, 4) their ideology, e.g. Simon the Zealot.

In the Bible, we find people or places named nearly 2,000 times, which indicates the importance of a name to the writers.

Nevertheless, there are times in the Bible when a name is just a name, and its meaning gives no additional insights to the passage, i.e. the long lists of names in Chronicles or names of places mentioned in Joshua and Judges, unless there is something in the context to demand a comment on the name's meaning.

GIVING A NAME IMPARTS AUTHORITY

Biblically, giving a name to someone showed authority over another (Isa. 43:1), while the naming of something or someplace declared your authority over it.

So, in the first chapters of Genesis we find that God *"called the light Day, and the darkness He called Night"* (1:5); *"He called the firmament*

Names were found inscribed on various items to indicate ownership, like this arrowhead which shows its owner to be, "Ada, son of Ba'l'a."

Heaven" (1:8); *"He called the dry land Earth"* and *"the waters He called Seas."* (1:10). God also created Man, and named him (1:26). God retained dominion over the things He named: the Heavens, Time, Land, Seas, and even Man.

However, God gave Man dominion over the creatures of the earth. Therefore, He had Adam name each one, thus conferring Man's authority over the things He gave to Man to manage.

"And out of the ground the Lord God formed every beast of the field, and every fowl of the air, and brought them unto Adam to see what he would call them; and whatsoever Adam called every living creature, that was the name thereof" (2:19).

There are occasions when God even renamed people in the Bible to impart His authority and character over His calling for them, e.g. Abram to Abraham (Gen. 17:5); Sarai to Sarah (Gen. 17:15); Jacob to Israel (Gen. 32:28); Simon to Peter (Mk. 3:16), etc.

USING A NAME APPROPRIATES AUTHORITY AND RESPONSIBILITY

In the Bible, to be given the name of another meant to pass on ownership, as when God gave His name to Israel (Dt. 28:9-10), or in the New Testament, when a person is baptized into the name of God (Mt. 28:19; Acts 8:16; I Cor. 1:13,15).

To be given the name of another meant to pass on authority and responsibility. The tradition of a wife taking the name of her husband confers his authority to her, and his responsibility for her.

To be sent to speak in someone's name, meant to go in his authority (Jer. 11:21; II Cor. 5:20). Moreover, one who goes on a mission in the Lord's name receives a blessing, *"Blessed is He who comes in the name of the Lord!"* (Jn. 12:13).

To pray in the name of God is to invoke His authority to the prayer: *"And whatever you ask in My name, that I will do... If you ask anything in My name, I will do it."* (Jn. 14:13,14).

Throughout the Scriptures, we see people using "the name of the Lord," (His authority), to appropriate His power into a situation for protection (Dt. 28:10; Ps.116:4; Ps. 124:8; Prov. 18:10), healing (Acts 3:6; Jas. 5:14), and other miracles (I Kgs. 18:24).

When David went up against Goliath, he pitted simple faith in the authority of the Lord against all of Goliath's man-made weapons, *"Then said David to the Philistine, 'You come to me with a sword, and with a spear, and with a shield: but I come to you in the name of the Lord of Hosts, the God of the armies of Israel, who you have defied'"* (I Sam. 17:45).

People also called upon "the name of the Lord" at times of indecision or great distress, seeking His guidance or intervention. *"Some trust in chariots, and some in horses; but we will remember the name of the Lord our God"* (Ps. 20:7). Salvation comes by calling upon the name of the Lord (Acts 2:21; Rom. 10:13).

THERE IS POWER IN THE NAME OF THE LORD

There is power in the authority of one's name, especially God's.

In the natural, we have all experienced how easy it is to get something done if someone of stature endorses you or your project and allows you to use their name, which represents their authority, character and reputation. Doors, which might otherwise be closed, can be opened. In Israel, this is called "proteksia."

This is also true of God's name. His name is so great, powerful and infallible, that in the Bible, it is recorded that He swore by His own name, to make the point that what He desired to do was absolutely guaranteed (Jer. 44:26).

However, it was, and is, possible to use God's name incorrectly. Readers of the Bible are warned about using God's name in vain. *"You shall not take the name of the Lord your God in vain, for the Lord will not hold him guiltless who takes His name in vain."* (Ex. 20:7; Dt. 5:11). One should not swear falsely by God's name nor profane it (Lev. 19:12), for blaspheming His name will result in death (Lev. 24:16), if not physical, then surely spiritual.

Even if God's name is invoked for selfish reasons, the power and authority of His name can still complete the transaction. However, misuse of God's name can bring serious repercussions.

Matthew 7:22-23 makes this point very clearly, *"Many will say to Me in that day, 'Lord, Lord, have we not prophesied in Your name, cast out demons in Your name, and done many wonders in Your name?'"* While it is obvious from this verse that incredible things were accomplished in the spiritual realm by invoking God's name, these people do not really know God! The following verse says, *"And then will I profess unto them, 'I never knew you; depart from me, you who work iniquity.'"*

Don't think this too strange. In the natural, this would be the same as using someone's name, without permission, to get something. You may get what you want in the short run. However, when the person discovers that you used his name, then you will have to pay the consequences. The commandment against taking God's name in vain literally means "do not carry God's name lightly or superficially."

We who are called by the name of the Lord need to be very careful how we are representing Him. Don't wear a T-shirt saying "In God We Trust" if you are not walking in a way that honors Him.

THE CHARACTER OF ONE'S NAME

Besides conferring authority, the Hebraic use of a name often depicts the character of a person or place.

Jacob (supplanter, replacer) became synonymous with one who is a deceiver, and this characteristic was found in his life. God changed his name to Israel (Gen. 32:28), meaning "prince of God" or "wrestled with God," to change his calling and his character.

After Achan was discovered to have been the one who brought sin into the camp of the Israelites near Jericho, he was taken to the Valley of Achor (trouble) where he was stoned to death. There, Joshua asked him, "Why have you troubled us?" The name, Achor, attests to Achan's "trouble." A curse was put on this place that will remain until Messiah comes (Isa. 65:10).

In the Bible, there is the closest possible relationship between a person and his name. To remove one's name is to extinguish that person's identity (Num. 27:4; Dt. 7:24; 12:3; Josh. 7:9; Ps. 9:5); or to forget a name breaks a relationship, e.g. to forget God's name is to depart from Him (Jer. 23:27).

To pray in the Name of the Lord is also praying in His character. What we ask and expect should be consistent with God's will and God's Word.

When people hear your name, what do they think about? Generally, what comes to mind is your character, your reputation, which they associate with your name. Therefore, God tells us, *"A good name is better than precious ointment"* (Ecc. 7:1).

THE NAMES OF GOD

Knowing that the Hebraic use of a name confers authority and character helps us. It is now easy to understand why God called Himself by different names at different times. Each imparted a special characteristic of the Lord which was needed in a given situation.

In the Hebrew Scriptures, there are 16 names God uses for Himself. There are also 13 names used for the Holy Spirit, and 117 names to refer to Messiah.

As Christians, we are certainly interested in Jesus's Hebrew name, Yeshua. The angel Gabriel, a messenger of the Lord, appeared to Joseph and told him of Mary, *"Joseph, son of David, do not be afraid to take Mary home as your wife, because what is conceived in her is from the Holy Spirit. She will give birth to a son, and you are to give Him the name, Yeshua, because He will save His people from their sins"* (Mt. 1:20-

The name of Yeshua in ancient Hebrew script.

21). Yeshua means "God saves," or Savior. His title is Meshiach, or Messiah, meaning "Anointed One." In Greek, the Hebrew name and title, Yeshua HaMeshiach, have come to us as Jesus Christ.

We also know that in fulfillment of a Messianic prophecy, a virgin would conceive and bear a son who would be called Immanuel, meaning

"*God with us*" (Isa. 7:14). This reference was cited in the Gospels with reference to Yeshua (Mt. 1:23), and is certainly a description of His character and His role.

Isaiah also describes Messiah with several names to show His authority and character in Isaiah 9:6, "*For unto us a Child is born, unto us a Son is given; and the government will be upon His shoulder, and His name will be called Wonderful Counselor, Mighty God, the Everlasting Father, the Prince of Peace.*"

Yeshua was born in Bethlehem (Lk. 2:4), meaning "House of Bread," and later referred to Himself as "*the Bread of Life*" (Jn. 6:35).

THE NAMES FOR ISRAEL

God also chose and named His land, Israel, which He claims as His own (Lev. 25:23). He gave this land in covenant to Abraham, Isaac and Jacob, and their descendants as an everlasting possession (Gen. 17:7-8).

It was here that He promised His continual presence and chose Jerusalem as His City for His eternal purposes, and claimed it with His name. "*The Lord said, 'In Jerusalem I will put my name'*" (II Kgs. 21:4).

Throughout the ages, men have tried to take this land away from the Jewish people by conquering the land and attempting to change its name. But ultimately, these efforts have failed, because of God's covenant and His faithfulness to it.

This is an important issue, when we consider the political conflict that exists today over the use of the names Palestine or Israel.

Let's look at the name Israel, which is found in the Bible 2,566 times!

Prior to biblical times, no one name specifically denoted the land of Israel. The early Egyptians used the terms Metenu and Hurru, each encompassing both Israel and its surrounding areas; from the late 14th to the 12th century BC, the term Kena'an, "the Land of Canaan," was used.

The name Eretz Yisrael, Hebrew for "the Land of Israel," was first employed at the time of the Israelite conquest to designate the land which, according to the Bible, was promised by God as an inheritance to the Israelite tribes. Another term that was widespread at that time was Eretz ha-Ivrim, "The Land of the Hebrews." It was also descriptively called the Holy Land, the Land of Milk and Honey, and the Promised Land.

When the kingdom of David and Solomon was divided in the 10th century BC, the name Yisrael (Israel) was restricted to the northern kingdom; the kingdom of the Davidic dynasty was known as Eretz Yehuda (the land of Judah) with its capital in Jerusalem.

After the Assyrian Exile (8th century BC), when the Israelite population that remained in the country was concentrated in Yehuda, the term Yehudi became a synonym for Israelite and Hebrew, hence the English term "Jew." After the return of the Jews from exile in Babylon, Yehuda was the name of the autonomous area of Jewish settlement and later of the Hasmonean and Herodian kingdoms.

ISRAEL IS NOT PALESTINE

The Greeks called the land Ioudaia and the Romans, Judaea, until the Second Jewish Revolt of the Jews against the Romans, the Bar-Koch-ba Revolt (132-135 AD), after which the Roman Emperor Hadrian changed its name to Palaestina. The name Palaestina was originally an adjective derived from Philistia, the area inhabited by the Philistines, the arch-enemies of Israel.

The Romans also changed the name of Jerusalem to Aelia Capitolina (after the family name of the conquering Emperor Hadrian), and only allowed the Jews to enter one day per year to mourn the destruction of the Temple.

These names were carefully chosen by the Romans to make a point. They wanted to erase God's chosen names for His land and city, and thus the connection between the Land and the Jewish people as given to them in covenant by God.

In the context of what we have learned in this letter about names, you can see how the name change by the Romans would be a constant reminder that absolute Roman authority and character would prevail over the region. Also, to have had the land and city renamed for the Jews' ancient and cur-rent enemies was like rubbing salt in their wounds of defeat.

Jar handle bearing two seal impressions, "Nera, son of Shibna," and "To the King - Hebron."

Throughout the New Testament, while province names are used for the land, e.g. Galilee, Judea and Samaria, the term used for the entire region is Israel, not Palestine. That came later.

Nevertheless, you often hear Christians referring to the Land of Palestine where Jesus lived. It did not get that name until 100 years after the death and resurrection of Yeshua, and when it did, it was for all the wrong reasons. To continue to use that name is to perpetuate the denial of God's covenants and purposes for this land.

During the Byzantine era, Palestine was the accepted name of the land, but the Jews in Israel and the Diaspora retained the name Eretz Yisrael, as well as ha-Eretz (the Land), terms which became permanently rooted in the consciousness of the Jewish people.

The Arabs considered the land to be a region of greater Syria, not a distinct country, and referred only to the names of specific towns. The Crusaders used the name Palestine, or "the Kingdom of Jerusalem." The name Palestine was also used by the British.

On May 14, 1948, the Jewish-held part of western Palestine was given the name Medinat Yisrael (the State of Israel) in the Declaration of Independence. The Arab-inhabited part of western Palestine was annexed to the Hashemite Kingdom of Jordan and was called the West Bank, and a strip to the southwest came under Egyptian military rule and was termed the Gaza Strip.

Today, the Palestinian Authority is claiming land in this region and plans on establishing a State of Palestine on land that, biblically, was given to Israel by God. You can see why there is such a conflict in the hearts of many biblicists, both Jews and Christians, over yielding sovereignty of this territory that has a prior divine claim.

WHAT DOES THIS ALL MEAN TO US?

What lessons can we all learn and apply from this study, now that we have an understanding of the deeper meaning of names in God's Kingdom?

First: Now, when you read the Bible, pay careful attention to the meanings of the names of people and places being used, about that person's character or authority, as this will help you understand more about the situation being recounted.

Second: As people who have accepted God's call into His Kingdom, we need to be very careful how we represent the Lord. When people hear your name, about what do they think? Generally, what comes to mind is your character, your reputation, which they associate with your name. Our lives also tell a story and we need to be sure it is honoring to the Lord's name. II Timothy 2:19 tells us, *"The Lord knows those who are His, and let everyone who names the name of Messiah, depart from iniquity."* Our lives need to be above reproach so that we do not, in word or deed, profane or blaspheme the "name of the Lord."

Third: We need to be careful how we speak to others and about others. Name-calling can hurt. We can speak into someone's life blessing or cursing by how we label them. We all have our faults, and we all have our strengths. We need to discover the strengths in others and name them to that person and to others about that person, in order to build up their character. Whenever possible we should speak positively of others, avoiding the unkind name-calling we often hear people saying, e.g.: stupid, cheapskate, dummy, an idiot, a jerk, nerd, four-eyes, tinsel-teeth, big foot, etc. Such names diminish one's character, particularly if they reflect on one's personality or looks.

The Bible is quite pointed about this, *"And, whoever says to his brother, 'Raca!' shall be in danger of the council. But, whoever says, 'You fool!' shall be in danger of hell fire"* (Mt. 5:22). Raca (empty-headed) is a rare Aramaic name for an "airhead."

Fourth: Our walk with the Lord in righteousness qualifies us to have our names written in the Lamb's book of life (Rev. 21:27). Imagine, God even knows our name, which means He knows our character. As we are all "sinners saved by God's grace," we need to realize that when we accept the Lord, we are baptized "in the Name of the Lord." God sees us as redeemed from the authority and character of the world, into His authority and character.

This should bring us great comfort. We actually belong to the Lord and He has called each of us by name, which He records in His Book of Life. *"Fear not, for I have redeemed you; I have called you by your name; You are Mine!"* (Isa. 43:1).

Therefore, let it be said of all of us, *"Blessed is he who comes in the Name of the Lord."*

This Lesson from the Land of the Bible is found in our
Jerusalem Mosaic Video Series, Program #106,
along with other exciting features.
Please turn to page 186 to order your copy.

ARE YOU GUARDING YOUR GATES?

Chapter 4

I'll never forget my first impression of Jerusalem, when I first came here in 1977. Although I had never been to Israel before, I had accepted a job as the Administrator for the Spafford Children's Center, which is located high up on the Old City walls of Jerusalem, near Damascus Gate.

FIRST IMPRESSIONS

It was a cool, clear January afternoon when I arrived. By the time we traveled from the airport to the Damascus Gate, the sun was beginning to set.

Never having seen the Old City of Jerusalem before, I was immediately drawn in by the majesty and beauty of the city—her ancient walls illuminated by the setting sun, and the domed roofs becoming 3-D because of the long shadows. Street vendors were trying to make their last sales, calling out to the crowds of people who buzzed like a swarm of bees, in and out of the Damascus Gate. I could hear the call to prayer from the minaret of a nearby mosque, while church bells added to the din of activity.

What an exciting place. And, this was to be my new home!

I knew the location of the Spafford Center, and could see it jutting out above and within the old walls to my left. The taxi had left me, as vehicles cannot travel on the narrow, stepped alleyways of the Old City.

Damascus Gate

There I was, standing in awe of the sight before me. Just then, a donkey driver approached me for hire. Strapping my heavy suitcases onto this beast of burden, we proceeded through the Damascus Gate. In the midst of the 20th century, I felt I had gone back in time, back to Bible times.

43

Damascus Gate is the northernmost gate of the eight gates of the Old City. Like many gates, it was named for the destination of the road that began at this gate - Damascus.

It is a beautiful gate with high, iron-clad doors that were once closed each night to keep marauders out of the city.

As we entered the huge gateway, I noticed we had to zigzag to get into the Old City. It wasn't just a straight shot. You first took a sharp left, then after about 30 feet, you took a sharp right, exiting the gateway inside the walls of the Old City.

As I proceeded up a stone path to my new home, I wondered about this gate into the city of Jerusalem, David's city, the City of God.

THE ORIGINAL FUNCTIONS
OF THE CITY GATE

In ancient times, the city gate was the busiest place in the city. Near or just inside the gates, there were courtyards or a broadening of the street where much of the city's social, business and legal interaction took place. There is where we find the reading of the Law and proclamations taking place (Josh. 20:4; II Chr. 32:6; Neh. 8:1,3); where justice was administered as the elders judged legal cases and business transactions (Dt. 16:18; II Sam. 15:2, Amos 5:10-15); where news was exchanged and discussed (Gen. 19:1), and local gossip was spread (Ps. 69:12). It was a place where markets flourished, e.g. the Fish Gate (Neh. 3:3) or the Sheep Gate (Neh. 3:1) in Jerusalem, and where trading centers for imported items were established.

Prophets and priests delivered admonitions and pronouncements at the gates (Isa. 29:21; Amos 5:10: Jer. 17:19, etc.). Criminals were punished just outside the gates (I Kgs. 21:10, Acts 7:58). The city gate was even the place where one could attract the attention of the sovereign or dignitary (II Sam. 19:8; I Kgs. 22:10; Est. 2:19,21; 3:2). It was where strangers who were visiting the city passed the night, if they had no place to stay.

To be chosen as an elder to sit at the gate of the city was an honorable position (Prov. 31:23; Dan 2:49), although it became a curse for Lot, who chose to be an elder at the gate of Sodom where he compromised his stand for the Lord (Gen. 19:1).

The Old City Walls and Gates of Jerusalem.

DEFENDING THE CITY
OFTEN BEGAN AT THE GATES

Since the gates of a city were the only way in or out of the city, the large doors of the gateway, which were made of metal and wood (Ps. 107:16; Isa. 45:2) were secured at night with iron or wooden cross bars (I Kgs. 4:13; Neh. 3:13) for the protection of the inhabitants.

The main gate of each city was large enough for the entry of chariots and carts. It was carefully designed and built to deter the entrance of enemy soldiers, as this was the most vulnerable place in the walls of a city. The gates were often flanked by towers (II Sam. 18:24, 33) on which watchmen stood, day and night.

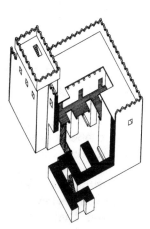

Some gates were built in a zigzag design, like the Damascus Gate in Jerusalem. This caused a man on horseback to slow down and open the defensive stance of his body as he maneuvered his horse through the passage, making it easier for defenders to kill him.

Other gates allowed straight passage into the city, like those of Solomon's great walled cities. They had multiple chambers in the passageway from which soldiers could attack

Solomonic Gate

intruders as a first line of defense, e.g. David awaited Absalom's army in one of these chambers (I Sam. 18:24). Most gates had vertical and horizontal openings, above and around the doors, through which to throw boiling liquids, spears, rocks, arrows and other sharp objects upon enemy soldiers. The Lord promised strength to those who turn back the battle at the gate (Isa. 28:6).

THE GATE SIGNIFIED AUTHORITY

In the Bible, the gate was more than the entrance and exit to a city. Figuratively, it represented the place of authority and the glory of the city (Isa. 3:26; Jer. 14:2). Like "fringes of the garment," which represented the authority of a man (see chapter 1), so too, the gate represented the place of authority of a city, where the elders sat. Scripture even refers to supernatural authority as the "gates of heaven" (Gen. 28:17) and the "gates of hell" (Mt. 16:18).

The biblical term, "to be within the gates," referred to being under the authority of the elders of the city who presided in the gates (Dt. 15:7; 31:12,13).

In battle, to "possess the gates" is a biblical term meaning to possess the city (Gen. 22:17; 24:60).

In the story of Samson, he took this quite literally. In his day, Israel

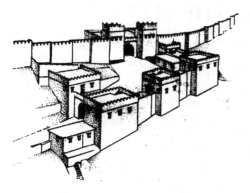

The main gate at Megiddo.

was under the control of the Philistines, a cruel and hateful people. Samson went down to the Philistine city of Gaza, where they had laid a trap for him and waited in the city gate to kill him. At midnight Samson tore their city gates, doorposts and cross bars from the walls of the city, (the symbol of their authority), and carried them off to Hebron, an Israelite city. This was a symbolic act of triumph for Israel and of humiliation for the Philistines (Jud. 16:2-3).

The Israelites were instructed to establish this authority with judges at the city gates (Dt. 16:18), as a place of judgment to insure justice and obedience to God's laws by the people.

Another function of the elders at the gate was to protect the city and their people from the outside world. The gate was the most vulnerable point in these ancient, walled cities, and it was necessary to place judges there to interview those entering the city to be sure their presence was welcomed. Evildoers who might cheat, steal or break the laws of the city were not allowed to enter or stay in the city (Dt. 17:2-5).

At Tel Dan, far to the north of the Hulah Valley in the tribal area of Dan, the main city gate was uncovered. There archaeologists found the seat of the chief elder, who sat on a throne-like platform with other elders to evaluate and interview those coming into the city, and also hear and judge the grievances of those within the city.

HONORING THE GATES
OF OUR HOMES AND OUR LIVES

You might ask, "How does this apply to me?"

Today, we live in open, unwalled cities. We have courts of law, and mayors and city councils who are seated at city hall, not at the city gate. Nevertheless, God's prescription to the Israelites and followers of the Bible to establish justice, is the basis of the legal systems in our Western societies today.

While we may not have any control over who enters our cities today, we personally do have that authority in our own homes, which God places under our authority.

You see, the door of the home is also a gateway. In Hebrew, a gateway or doorway is the same word, sha'ar, and the Bible has much to say about our responsibility to keep the focus of our homes on the Lord.

Deuteronomy 11:18a-20a, says: *"Therefore you shall lay up these words of Mine in your heart and in your soul... you shall teach them to your children, speaking of them when you sit in your house, when you walk by the way, when you lie down, and when you rise up. And you shall write them on the doorposts of your house and on your gates, that your days and the days of your children may be multiplied..."*

Typical door Mezuzah.

Ever since Moses spoke these words, the Jewish people have literally placed God's Word on the gates of their cities and on the doorframes of their homes—on the doorframes of the entrances to the house and on the doors to each room in the house used for living purposes. The Scriptures from Deuteronomy 6:4-9 and 11:13-21 are rolled up and placed inside a *mezuzah*, which is a small metal, stone, wooden or ceramic box nailed on the right doorframe. Throughout the ages, faithful Jews have touched the *mezuzah* upon entering and exiting buildings, homes and individual rooms, which has the effect of keeping them focused on the Lord, whom they serve.

Believe me, paying that kind of attention to the Lord, if done sincerely, would cause you to consider deeply the kinds of activities and thoughts you would engage in.

We have a place of responsibility before God and to our families to uphold the precepts of God and "guard the gates" of our homes - guarding against negative outside influences that would detract from a God-centered environment (Dt. 17:2-5; 21:18-19). God will honor this commitment to Him.

A striking example of this is found in the story of Passover. Moses told the people to slay a lamb and place the blood on the doorpost and lintel of their home. Then the angel of death would pass over the door and not allow the destroyer to come into their houses to strike any who were in the home, Israelite or not. (Ex. 12:22-23). Those who obeyed were spared.

Being responsible over the "door" of our home also includes those who come into our home and how they behave.

Deuteronomy 31:12-13, says,

"Gather the people together, men and women and little ones, and the stranger who is within your gates, that they may hear and that they may learn to fear the LORD your God and carefully observe all the words of this law, and that their children, who have not known it, may hear and learn to fear the LORD your God as long as you live in the land which you cross the Jordan to possess."

Scripture portion placed in Mezuzah.

Some may think my wife, Pat, and I are old-fashioned, but when our daughters, Ashley and Allison, bring their friends into our home, their words and deeds are expected to be honoring to the Lord, even if they are not Bible-believers. God's values are honored in our home and Ashley and Allison's friends can see and hear this when visiting.

My observation, even in Jerusalem, is that often, Bible-believing children and teen-agers are easily swayed to speak and act like non-believers in the world, not the other way around. Sometimes it takes the loving encouragement of a parent to guide the situation into a pattern that honors the Lord.

Not only does "guarding the gate" involve who and what comes into the front or back door, but through other vulnerable access points, or gate-ways, into our home. This would include television, radio and even reading material. Just as the ancient elders of the cities of Israel were to keep unsavory things from entering the city to protect their people, we have that charge over our place of authority. The prophet Isaiah spoke sharply to Israel about the sinful practices that went on in their homes (Isa. 57:8)..

What are we watching on television, or listening to on the radio? What magazines and books enter our home? In a world that has moved far from the values of the Bible, it is easy to find the influences of the world creeping in upon us and chipping away at our biblical values, right in our own homes. A chip here and a chip there, and before you know it, we are guilty of the same sin as Israel, who flirted with the things of the world in opposition to the biblical precepts of God.

That spelled disaster for ancient Israel, and it will spell disaster for us, as well. None of us is immune, and we find we have to be a true "watchman at the gate" of our home, daily. Old-fashioned or not, I find it exciting to take a stand and glorify the Lord in our home, bringing up our children in the *"nurture and admonition of the Lord"* (Eph. 6:4), and then watching how the Lord blesses this effort. For those of us who are parents, it is our responsibility to *"train up a child in the way he should go, and when he is old he will not depart from it"* (Prov. 22:6). This all begins in our homes.

Finally, out of our mouths come forth what is in our hearts. Your words will reveal your heart which speaks evil, or righteousness that leads to salvation (Mt. 15:18; Lk. 6:45; Rom. 10:10). Our mouth is the "gateway" that proclaims what is really going on in our lives. So the Psalmist cries out to the Lord, *"Set a guard, O LORD, over my mouth; Keep watch over the door of my lips"* (Ps. 141:3). The Lord expects us, with His help, to guard every aspect of our lives under our authority.

SETTING UP THE DEFENSES

Just as the ancient walled cities defended their inhabitants against the "enemy" who would seek to destroy them, we need to stand guard in our home and guard our lips for the Lord.

Just as the gate was configured in a way to deter outside attack, so we need to be prepared, through prayer and action, to protect those "within our gates," our families and those who visit us. We need to set a standard and stick with it so that we can defend our families from ungodly, unbiblical influences.

Matthew uses the image of the gate to express how we need to conduct our lives, *"Enter by the narrow gate; for wide is the gate and broad is the way that leads to destruction, and there are many who go in by it"* (Mt. 7:13).

How do we do this?

I am not suggesting we turn our homes into a legalistic, dogmatic, protective fortress enforced by the "laying down of the law" by an authoritarian figurehead.

I am speaking of establishing a biblical home environment that imparts the love, joy and wisdom of the Lord through following biblical values. Then, when compared with the standard of the world, a home set apart for the Lord will prove itself to be the "higher ground" that will be sought after by your family and friends. And it will produce the fruit of righteousness for the Lord.

My wife, Pat, as a teen-age baby sitter, worked in a Christian home where the love of the Lord was expressed on a daily basis, and that contact eventually brought her to the Lord. At this point in our family life, our children are young and we are appreciating this time when we can gently build godly values into their hearts. We know times of testing will come later and appreciate your prayers for our family as we pray for yours.

Let's encourage each other in creative ways to protect the gates of our homes and hearts. We can impart the Lord within our gates, rather than simply letting the world take over via TV, video, radio, the Internet, and magazines, and by the people who visit there.

Let's be pro-active like the elders at the gate. Check out who and what comes into your home and make it a little corner of the Kingdom of God that attracts others because of the joy, life and light of God that is expressed there. In a world that is searching for meaning, purpose and inner fulfillment, they may find it in our homes.

After all, God created us and then gave us His Word as a guide for our lives so we can live it more abundantly. If we do so and prove that it works, then God will be glorified in our lives, as He should be.

We who dwell in the Kingdom of God need to live righteously and thankfully before the Lord. To be found in His presence, "within His gate," we will have joy and gladness.

"This is the gate of the LORD, through which the righteous shall enter" (Ps. 118:20).

"Enter into His gates with thanksgiving, and His courts with praise. Be thankful to Him, and bless His name" (Ps.100:4).

This Lesson from the Land of the Bible is found in our
Jerusalem Mosaic Video Series, Program #113,
along with other exciting features.
Please turn to page 186 to order your copy.

LIVING IN THE DAYS OF THE BIBLE

Chapter 5

When I was a child, one of my favorite television programs was called "You Are There!" This was a history series that took the viewer back in time to various historical periods to meet important figures and "put you in the picture."

I have never met a person who is not interested in knowing what it was like to live in days gone by. For Christians and Jews, this is particularly true if that past is the lifestyle of the Bible. Most of us have heard Bible stories all of our lives. Many of these stories give us a glimpse into the life of the characters. However, most of the biblical accounts assume a knowledge already understood by the writers and by those to whom they were writing. Sadly, we have lost much of this background which can enliven our Bible reading immensely.

For this reason, I want to "put you into the biblical scene" so you can get a feel for what it was like to live in the days of the Bible. I will be using some research compiled by a colleague, Gordon Brubacher. We hope you enjoy this study.

Before we can look at the details of everyday life in the Bible, we must appreciate the underlying background upon which this daily life was played. This background is not something that can be shown, because it is not tangible. Nor was it described in great detail in written texts, because it was assumed that everyone understood it. But with a little research, we too can understand it today.

The ancient City of David was the size of a small village.

51

You see, this background is the feelings and emotional reactions that people felt when faced with the challenges of everyday life - a life very different from our own today.

The paramount feeling that motivated the people of the Bible was fear and insecurity; fear that one might not survive until tomorrow or next year, along with hope that somehow you might.

SURVIVAL WAS THE KEY

During the biblical period in the Land of Israel, many things threatened life and made it fragile. Survival was a major effort and it occupied a great deal of time and attention. Life was different than it is in our modern, industrialized society of today. Because we are more secure, we expect to live not only tomorrow, but to a ripe old age. Whether this is an illusion or not, this mindset prevents us from appreciating the daily peril that gripped those living 2,000-4,000 years ago.

The threat that prevailed was on two levels: 1) individual: "Will I, myself, live until tomorrow or next year?"; and, 2) communal: "Will my group (family, clan, village, town, city, tribe, nation) survive at all?"

In today's industrialized societies which are highly organized to protect the nation and care for society as a whole, national survival is often taken for granted. Today, we are able to be more preoccupied with our individual well-being. However, in the biblical period, the survival of the nation or community was often more important to consider than individual survival. It was not a question of *if* an invading army, plague, famine or drought was coming, but *when*.

The threats were of two kinds: natural and human.

WHAT WERE THE NATURAL THREATS?

Just consider life with no doctors, no medicine, no public health, no hospitals, and no surgery. The lack of many of these things we take for granted today created a potentially lethal environment in the days of the Bible. Consider this.

- **Mortality** rates for mothers and infants were high (e.g., II Sam. 12:21).

- **Illness**, without our cornucopia of medicines and wonder drugs, was lethal, and people were helpless to prevent death (e.g., Dt. 28:27; II Kgs. 20:1; Acts 12:21-23)

- **Injury** made everyone vulnerable. To break an arm or leg could mean maiming for life. This could take away your ability to provide for your family, to keep up with your group on the move, or to defend yourself or your family from other dangers. An injury from a sharp tool

A young boy accompanies his wounded father to the surgeon.

could get infected and, without medication and stitches, result in death by loss of blood, gangrene or tetanus. Again, there was nothing you could do about it.

- **Plague** threatened the community as a whole, whether family, clan, village, city or entire region (e.g., I Sam. 5).

- **Starvation** was always a possibility with an agricultural economy and subsistence farming. In a land of marginal rainfall, slight variations in rainfall resulted in poor crops or none at all. Crops and stores were also subject to pestilence, locust plagues (Nah. 3:15), and invading armies. Also food storage capabilities were limited to dry grains, and salting and drying processes, as no refrigeration was available. You could not go to your local supermarket to replenish your supplies. Even if grain or other foodstuffs were available in a neighboring region or nation, how much could you carry home in two sacks on your donkey? The result of crop failure, drought, or spoilage meant famine, sickness, malnutrition and death (e.g., Gen. 41:56; Ruth 1:1; II Sam 21:1). Faced with starvation, people were often forced to pack up and move in an effort to find water and food. This would be a difficult task without knowing where to go or how to get there in the quick, comfortable mode we enjoy today.

WHAT WERE THE HUMAN THREATS?

Human threats came from people who had the power to hurt you. These included an enemy army, those in authority over you, or even your neighbors. For this reason, you had to consider how to defend yourself from these perils.

- **War** was the primary human threat (e.g., II Kgs. 24:10). Geographically, the Land of Israel is located between the great powers of the ancient world and was the land bridge between the empires - Babylon, Anatolia (Hittite), Assyria, Mitanni (Hurrian), Aram, and Phoenicia at various times to the north and east; with Egypt and Philistia to the south and west; and Ammon, Moab, and Edom to the south and east. The Bible is full of accounts of war or impending wars between these powers with the Land of Israel caught in the middle.

Major roads passed through the land and were used by outside armies on the march. Israel found itself as a buffer zone between warring nations. At times Israel itself was the target of direct attack, not to mention civil war

Occupying powers, as in the pictured Assyrian invasion, were an ever present threat.

between the Northern and Southern Kingdoms during the period of the Divided Monarchy after Solomon.

Armies marched through constantly, taking what they pleased. First on their list was slaves, then treasure, provisions, etc. Those they did not take as slaves were killed or abused and left for dead. War not only affected the able-bodied men who were killed in battle. But what about the women and children on the losing side? Those who survived multiple rapes and beatings would starve if left behind, because the earth was most often scorched by the enemy.

- **Kings and Rulers** or those placed in authority by an occupying power were another human threat. This was not just on a national level, but included regional governors and local magistrates. Displeasing him could be fatal in a time when rulers had absolute power over your life and death. A particular problem was distrust of your loyalty. This threat would cause you to watch what you said, since even a jealous rival could tell the ruler you were disloyal, resulting in certain punishment and possibly death.

WHAT WERE THE RESPONSES TO THE NATURAL AND HUMAN THREATS TO YOUR LIFE?

- **Death:** One result was that you died. Many people perished before their time due to one or more threats that they could not overcome. The ancients had every reason to feel insecure about life.

- **Avoid trouble**: Just do your job, farm well, and make as few enemies as possible.

The Bible, as well as other writings from the ancient Near East, is full of advice for conducting one's life so as to stay out of trouble. It provides guidance for conforming to the principles which underlie society in general and also the universe as a whole. These instructions were given so you would not alienate the people and powers which could harm you. The Book of Proverbs, for example, is a virtual survival manual for many aspects of life and its potential dangers, as are instructions of the Law in Leviticus and Deuteronomy.

- **Complain to God:** More than 50 lament psalms are a cry to God in time of deep trouble, very often mentioning the threat of death. When they do so, they are not in mere figurative language, but a response to a real threat. The psalmists were in real danger for their lives in a world that was very fragile. (Cf. Ps. 13:4; 17:11-14; 18:4-6; 22:19-21; 30:1-3; 39:10).

- **People helped each other,** or at least they should have. In the Hebrew Scriptures (the Old Testament) it is important to notice who does or does not help others, and who is in need (e.g., Dt. 5:20; Isa. 41:6; Lk. 10:27). The prophets frequently made such failure to help others the target of their criticism (e.g., Prov. 14:21).

- **People looked for help from their rulers:** The big question for the rulers was: "Where shall we place our trust?" Internally, some answers were in keeping large grain and water storage facilities, big armies, lots of chariots, major fortifications, and an indigenous national defense (e.g., I Kgs. 9:15-19). Externally, a ruler worked to secure treaties and strategic alliances with other nations, particularly alignments with the superpower of the day, which he hoped proved to be the strongest; e.g., in the last twenty years of Judah, they changed alliances six times.

- **People found help or hope in the Divine Sphere:** Turning to a deity of some kind was not the option we have today. A secular lifestyle was not as prevalent because the threats that you faced caused you to seek divine intervention. Our self-sufficiency makes us feel secure and our modern society wrongly believes we do not need to turn to the divine. But the insecure ancients had a host of gods. However, each was limited in their power because they were idols of stone and clay - except for the God of Israel, the God of the Bible. Biblically, the correct response was to trust in the God of Israel who would provide divine protection and help. It should have been the first place for the rulers and people of Israel to turn. To receive divine protection from the God of Israel was guaranteed. However, there were ethical strings attached to expecting help from God (Cf. Lev. 26:3-10; Dt. 30:15-20; I Kgs. 8:33-40, 46-53).

On the one hand, in a world of pagan deities that were seen as whimsical and capricious, the God of Israel was forthright and revealed what was required to receive His blessing. This was seen as a comfort to the people of Israel and those who followed Him. No longer did one have to wonder if they were doing the right thing to appease "the gods." They knew exactly what to do to please the Lord. On the other hand, following God's Law took discipline and faith, which many lacked.

As is the case today, the average person in the biblical period often neglected this option, or worse, looked to pagan deities for help. This was a day when all deities were considered to be most effective in their own realm, and the God of Israel was seen by some as God of the Sinai Desert. The Canaanite god, Baal, was the god of rain, fertility and national

God's Word provided help and hope for the Israelites and those around them who chose to follow Him.

security, the definitive answers to the deepest natural fears and insecurities for life in the Land of Israel, former Canaan. Further, outside of general devotion to him, there were no ethical requirements in Baal worship.

For this reason, the Bible is full of accounts of the Israelites, including Israel's leaders at times, looking for the easy path of following the world around them. They strayed from God's law and His worship and turned to the deities of the nations around them, including Baal. The common man wanted rain and offspring, while the kings wanted national security.

In the end, the easy way was the wrong way, as the pagan gods were stone silent, and the people who forsook God lost His blessing and received His judgment.

INSTRUCTIONS FOR AN ABUNDANT LIFE

The Hebrew Scriptures and the New Testament (NT) are full of passages that give us the secret to the abundant life and protection and security from the Lord Himself.

When Solomon built his temple to the Lord, he prayed a prayer to the Lord. Included in this prayer was his appeal for God's protection for the people of Israel in accordance with their dependence upon the Lord:

"When famine or plague come to the land, or blight or mildew, locust or grasshoppers, or when an enemy besieges them in any of their cities, whatever disaster or disease may come, and when a prayer or plea is made by any of Your people Israel - each one aware of the afflictions of his own heart, and spreading out his hands toward this temple - then hear from heaven, Your dwelling place. Forgive and act; deal with each man according to all he does, since You know his heart (for You alone know the hearts of all men), so that they will fear You all the time they live in the land You gave our fathers" (I Kgs. 8:37-40).

God promises us His protection and provision if only we will get our priorities straight and look to Him as our Source. As humans, we allow our needs to take our eyes off the Lord and onto the need as we work to solve our own problems. However, the Scriptures tell us to look to the Lord first, and then He will solve those problems and do the providing.

Deuteronomy 28:1-14 told the ancients what blessings they could expect if they followed the Lord and His commandments. In the NT, Matthew tells us not to worry about our lives, what we will wear, what we will eat or drink, or where we will live. He concludes, *"For the pagans run after all these things and your heavenly Father knows that you need them. But seek first the kingdom of God and His righteousness, and all these things will be given to you as well"* (Mt. 6:32-33).

The key is seeking the Lord first and His righteousness. This Scriptural truth has not changed throughout the ages, for God is *"the same yesterday and today and forever"* (Heb. 13:8).

Let us not think that we are immune to the natural and human threats of life any more than our biblical ancestors. While we may have a safety net of security, plentiful goods and services, good nutrition and heath, medicine and hospitals that make these threats seem far away from us, in reality a threat to our life is only a breath away. James 4:14-15 confirms, *"Why, you do not even know what will happen tomorrow. What is your life? You are a vapor that appears for a little while and then vanishes. Instead, you ought to say, 'If it is the Lord's will, we will live and do this or that.'"*

Ultimately, we are as completely vulnerable and dependent upon the Lord as the ancients. We may *feel* as though we are the "masters of our own fate," but actually, our destiny rests in the hands of the Lord.

Let us not be fooled and distracted by all the "things" in our lives, no matter how good they are. Many of them are good and true blessings given to us by the Lord. Yet, if they get in the way and take our attention away from Him as first priority, then we will miss out on the abundant life the Lord has for us.

We too are living in the days of the Bible, and the answer to the threats of life is the same today as it has been throughout the ages. Let us run into the presence of the Lord and live by His Word. There we can experience the true abundance of spiritual life, as we enjoy the abundance He also provides for us in our physical life.

All that is left for us to do is to respond to Him by faith. Yeshua told us, *"I have come that they may have life, and have it more abundantly"* (Jn. 10:10).

It is ours for the taking. Let's accept the Lord's offer today.

This Lesson from the Land of the Bible is found in our
Jerusalem Mosaic Video Series, Program #104,
along with other exciting features.
Please turn to page 186 to order your copy.

THE PASSOVER - LAST SUPPER CONNECTION

Chapter 6

For English-speaking Christians, the understanding of the connection between Passover and Easter is often vague, at best. In most European languages, however, the name for Resurrection Sunday is derived from the Hebrew word for Passover, *"Pesach."* However, in English, the term we use, Easter, is derived from the Anglo-Saxon pagan goddess of Spring, *Eostre*, whose festival, called Eastre, came at the spring equinox.

By the time Christianity reached the shores of merry ol' England, the Church had already lost much of its Old Testament Hebraic roots. It is sadly understandable how the Church could equate the resurrection and new life with an already practiced pagan spring festival of new life and fertility. It made the message more palatable to the masses, but this compromise allowed pagan practices to continue which diluted the faith. The Church allowed the incorporation of pagan fertility symbols of brightly-colored Easter eggs and rabbits, while adding the custom of preparing yeast-raised, hot cross buns to be eaten on Good Friday ... apparently oblivious that this is the Feast of Unleavened Bread when one eats flat matza without yeast!

This process of incorporating pagan symbols into the Church while cutting away its Hebraic roots was prevalent throughout Church history. Thus, all kinds of distortions of interpretation crept into the Church's understanding of Scripture, particularly when it

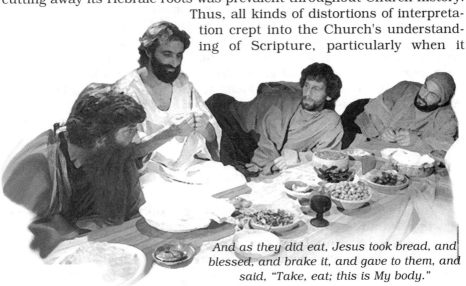

And as they did eat, Jesus took bread, and blessed, and brake it, and gave to them, and said, "Take, eat; this is My body."

incorporated pagan cultures which compromised the original meaning.

Concerning the Passover - Last Supper connection, the severing of that relationship goes back to the early days of the Church. From the 2nd century AD, some of the early Church Fathers made pronouncements against the Jews and opposed Christians participating in the celebration of Passover. For instance, Ignatius, Bishop of Antioch, spoke of the Passover in this way, "If anyone celebrates the Passover along with the Jews or receives emblems of their feast, he is a partaker with those who killed the Lord and His apostles." It is this kind of teaching which perpetrated Christian anti-Semitism. It is vital that we make sure this kind of thinking is not in our subconscious, as we come to learn of the Passover.

Let us not make the same error. As we study Passion Week and the remembrance of the Last Supper, the event in time when we Christians received the institution of the Communion from Yeshua (Jesus) Himself, we need to re-examine our roots:

"On the first day of the Feast of Unleavened Bread, the disciples came to Jesus and asked, 'Where do You want us to make preparations for You to eat the Passover?' He replied, 'Go into the city to a certain man and tell him, 'The Teacher says: My appointed time is near. I am going to celebrate the Passover with My disciples at your house.' So the disciples did as Jesus had directed them and prepared the Passover" (Mt. 26:17-19).

When we consider the New Testament references, we discover something quite different from what the early Church Fathers taught regarding the keeping of the biblical feasts. We see that Yeshua and all His disciples kept the festivals. They apparently not only kept the major pilgrimage festivals, but it seems Yeshua Himself even kept the lesser non-Biblical festivals like Hanukkah, or the Feast of Dedication (Jn. 10:22). In the Scripture, we learn that Yeshua "desired" to keep the Passover with His disciples (Lk. 22:15). Later on in Christian tradition, we hear the Apostle Paul charging Gentile Christians to *"keep the feast"* (I Cor. 5:8). Paul himself clearly kept the Jewish festivals and on one occasion sought to arrive in Jerusalem for the Feast of Pentecost (Acts 20:16).

The purpose of these biblical feasts was to help the people of God keep the miracle stories of God alive and remembered. They can still serve as learning tools for us today. So, let us examine and compare the Feasts of Israel in relation to the Passion Week of Yeshua and Pentecost, in order to discover the deeper meaning behind these significant events in the Church, particularly the communion, as we look at them from a Hebraic perspective.

THE PASSOVER AND CHRISTIANS

In recent years, Christians have had an increasing interest in this ancient celebration. This may be surprising when we consider Christian history and the continual efforts to put a wedge between the Church and the Jewish people, with some "New Testament Christians," even today, disregarding the Old Testament as a message from the past that has no value to Christianity. Interestingly, Yeshua Himself spoke on this matter and said, *"Do not think I have come to destroy the Law and the Prophets; I have not come to abolish them, but to fulfill them"* (Mt. 5:17-18). Yeshua's appearance on earth was within a historical context, in fulfillment of God's redemptive plan, which promised the means for the salvation of the world. Often, we Christians interpret Yeshua and His message out of context, thereby losing much understanding.

The rift between Christianity and its Jewish roots began shortly after the destruction of the Temple in 70 AD and the end of Jewish sovereignty in Jerusalem. A deep rivalry and suspicion began to develop between Gentile Church leaders and the Jewish people. Moves were made in the early Church to discredit Judaism and usurp Judaism's position as a legal religion in the Roman Empire; a right not granted to Christianity. This happened in spite of the fact that from the very beginning of Christianity, Judaism and Jewish believers in Yeshua had played a crucial role in the development of the infant Church.

An example of this rivalry and suspicion can be seen in the controversy over the date of celebrating Resurrection Sunday. In the early years of the Church, this day had been rightly celebrated according to the Jewish lunar calendar in conjunction with the week of Passover. However, at the Council of Nicea in 325 A.D., the Church chose a new method of dating the celebration, cutting it away from its Hebraic roots.

Paul, in Romans and Ephesians, makes it clear that we Christians have a shared covenant with Israel. In Romans 11:16-24, Paul talks about the wild olive branches being grafted among the natural branches into the olive tree that grows out of a holy root. The root is the Messiah, the Word of God, which is holy and provides the sap that nourishes the branches (v. 18). The tree is the covenants and promises made to Israel. Israel is the natural branches, and the Church is the wild branches sanctified by the sap and grafted into the covenants and promises, being joint-heirs with Israel. We *"become a partaker with them of the root and fatness of the olive tree,"* which God established. We are a part of something that pre-existed the Church, the Jewish people, of whom Paul tells us to honor and bless (Rom. 11:18). (See chapter 1)

In Ephesians, the apostle says that we were once *"aliens from the commonwealth of Israel, and strangers from the covenants of promise, having no hope, and without God in the world"* (Eph. 2:12). Now, however, *"in Christ Jesus we are made near by the blood"* of the Lamb (v. 13). We are no longer *"strangers and foreigners, but fellow citizens with the saints and of the household of God."* (v. 19).

As Christians, we now share in the covenants, the promises, the festivals - and yes, even the Passover. We now have the privilege of sharing all these festivals with Israel. There are books in your Christian bookstore on how Christians can celebrate and appreciate the lessons of the biblical feasts, which you can use at home. However, for a more meaningful experience, joining a Passover seder meal with a Jewish family or at a local synagogue can be very enlightening. Christians can gain much from this experience as we learn of God's faithfulness to the Children of

Israel as He brought them out of Egypt. While there are many lessons for Christians to learn from celebrating Jewish holidays, it is also important to let Jewish people define their own holidays for us.

Some Christians object that the Passover and other Levitical feasts have no significance for New Testament believers. However, this is clearly not the case as we see in Leviticus 23:21. The Passover as well as the other pilgrim festivals are described as *"statutes forever."* We see a confirmation of this in Zechariah 14:16, where it is said that the nations will someday come to Jerusalem to celebrate the Feast of Tabernacles. Even Yeshua said regarding the Passover cup, that He would someday drink of it anew with His disciples in His Father's kingdom (Mk. 14:25).

PREPARATIONS FOR THE PASSOVER

Let's look at the order of the Passover more closely. The week of Passover actually encompasses three Feasts of Israel mentioned in Leviticus 23: Passover (Pesach), Unleavened Bread, and First Fruits.

The search for "chametz"

A Passover meal is eaten on the eve of the first day of Passover. This meal is referred to as the "seder." In Hebrew, the word "seder" means "order." In modern Hebrew, we often hear the word "beseder" for OK. It literally means, "in order."

The Passover meal is organized in stages to insure that all the elements of the Passover blessings, recognition of the Passover foods and symbols, and the retelling of the story of the exodus of the Children of Israel from Egypt, are included. The "seder" was established over 3,500 years ago and has not changed appreciably in the past 2,000 years, to insure that the story of what God did for His people was passed on from generation to generation, according to the injunction to do so in Exodus 13:8.

There is not only an order in eating the meal, but also in the manner of preparation for the Passover. In Matthew 26:17-19, Yeshua sent His disciples to make preparation for their last Passover meal together.

What kind of preparation was necessary? Actually, the preparation for Passover is quite involved and can go on for days preceding the holiday. It involves, first of all, a thorough cleaning of the house, especially the kitchen, and all areas related to food service. During this festival week, only "matza" (unleavened bread) can be eaten and all leaven must be purged from your house. After all cleaning is finished, a symbolic search for that last remaining crumb of "chametz" (leaven) is conducted by the father and his sons on the day before Passover. He searches the house with a candle, brushes up that last remaining bit of leaven with a feather, and then destroys it.

Throughout Israel, for the whole feast period of Passover and Unleavened Bread, grocery stores will not sell leavened items of any kind. All this is in response to the command, *"For seven days no yeast (leavening) is to be found in your houses. And whoever eats anything with yeast in it must be cut off from the community of Israel, whether he is a stranger or native-born...Wherever you live you must eat unleavened bread"* (Ex. 12:19, 20b).

When the Jewish people refrain from eating food with leavening and only eat matza for seven days, they are physically reminded of the meaning of leavening and the need to purge it. It leaves a lasting impression.

As Christians, this preparation should teach us many lessons. There is a spiritual preparation which is surely reflected here. The Apostle Paul in I Corinthians 5:7-8 challenges us to, *"Purge out the old leaven, that you might be a new lump, as you are unleavened. For even Christ our Passover is sacrificed for us: Therefore let us keep the feast, not with old leaven, neither with the leaven of malice and wickedness; but with the unleavened bread of sincerity and truth."*

In the Bible, leaven represents evil and wickedness. The clear point is that God wants evil out of our lives. The Gospel not only brings salvation but also sanctification (purification). The latter is a process which must go on every day of our lives.

It is in this vein that Paul speaks concerning the manner in which we should take communion, *"A man ought to examine himself before he eats of the bread and drinks of the cup"* (I Cor. 11:28).

There is another matter of spiritual preparation which we need to make for the Passover. In Leviticus 23:8 it is commanded that no servile work may be done on the Passover. In other words, no burdens may be borne on this or the other pilgrimage festivals.

When we celebrate Passover, we should pray at the beginning that God may lift heavy burdens from the hearts of the celebrants. After all, Passover is the festival of our freedom - freedom from the slavery and drudgery of sin.

We should especially invite the Spirit to be present, because the Bible says that *"where the Spirit of the Lord is, there is liberty"* (II Cor. 3:17). Traditionally, celebrants may assume a relaxed pose and even recline on pillows, signifying that they are no longer slaves but free people.

LIGHTING OF
THE FESTIVAL CANDLES

On Passover eve, one of the first responsibilities is the lighting of the Festival candles. The Festival candles are lit and blessed by the woman of the house. This custom has

probably been carried down in tradition as a reminder of the great Meno-
rah which once stood in the Temple. In that sense, the candles may well
represent the Holy Spirit, God's presence both in the Temple, and in the
Church. As Christians, we need to reflect that it was a woman, Mary,
who gave birth to Yeshua, the Light of the World.

THE PASSOVER FOODS

Along with the spiritual preparation is the physical preparation.
Our God is a "show and tell" God. Therefore, this meal is a special meal
with specific foods that remind us of the many miracles God performed
when He delivered the Israelites from the land of Egypt. This helps in the
retelling of the Exodus story from one generation to the next. Along with
the special foods, there is also a banquet for this celebration for freedom.
An elder of the family usually presides over the seder meal to keep it moving through the retelling of the Exodus story, leading the prayers, explain-
ing the food elements, and making sure nothing is forgotten.

In the Second Temple period, the people generally ate foods locally
grown in the land of Israel. While there was trade and some imported food
was available, it was expensive and not affordable to most. However, on a
special occasion such as this, some imported spices would certainly have
been used.

Local foods were served at a first century Passover meal: dried
fruits: e.g. figs, raisins, dates, dried apricots; vegetables: carrots, cucum-
bers, celery, parsley; olives and pickles; nuts: almonds, walnuts, and
carob; stuffed grape leaves; roasted eggs; honey; rice with pine nuts; lamb
stew, called the sop; olive oil; unleavened bread; diluted wine.

On the seder table, there is a seder plate with various foods. Some
are eaten and others are there to remind the participants to recount the
entire miraculous Exodus event.

The Four Cups Of Wine

There are four cups of diluted sweet wine that are drunk during the
meal as the story unfolds.

1) The first cup, drunk at the beginning of the meal, is called the
Cup of Sanctification.

2) The second cup is the Cup of Judgment,
drunk during the reciting of the story of the Exodus at the place where the plagues are recited.
(Blood - Frogs - Lice - Flies - Cattle Disease - Boils
- Hail - Locust - Darkness - Death of the Firstborn). As each plague is mentioned, the people dip
in their finger and take out a drop of wine,
because a full cup represents fullness of joy, and
no one should be joyful over the judgments that
befell the Egyptians —

3) The third cup is the Cup of Redemption,

drunk after the meal, and —

4) The fourth cup is called the Cup of Praise, drunk at the end of the whole meal, after a time of singing the Hallel Psalms 115-118. It is a time of celebration over God's deliverance from bondage and sin.

In addition to the names and timing of these four cups, they are based on the four "I wills" of Exodus 6:6-7, and each of these four cups has a name associated with it. In order, these four cups are called: 1) The Cup of Sanctification, *"I will bring you out from under the burdens of the Egyptians...,"* 2) The Cup of Judgment, *"I will rid you out of their bondage...,"* 3) The Cup of Redemption, *"I will redeem you with a outstretched arm...,"* and, 4) The Cup of Praise, *"I will take you to Me for a people."*

Before drinking each of these cups, a traditional Hebrew blessing is said: *Ba-ruch A-ta A-do-nai El-ohei-nu Me-lek ha-o-lam bo-ree pree ha-ga-fen.* This means, "Blessed art Thou, O Lord our God, King of the universe, Who created the fruit of the vine."

In the Hebrew culture, one's eyes are open looking up to heaven to thank God who is our Creator and Provider.

At every Passover meal, there was a cup set on the table for the hoped-for Elijah, who would come in fulfillment of prophecy and reveal the Messiah. This made the Passover meal the occasion of Messianic expectation.

Matzah (Unleavened Bread)

Matzah is the unleavened bread. Leavening represents sin, and during this entire Passover week, all foods containing leavening must be purged out of the house. As Christians, we can see that Yeshua's unleavened, sinless life is an example for our lives.

In the seder story, what does the *matzah* represent? It means that the dough of our fathers did not have opportunity to become leavened before the King of Kings, the Holy One, Blessed is He, revealed Himself to them and redeemed them. As it is said, *"And they baked unleavened cakes of the dough which they brought forth out of Egypt, for it was not leavened, because they were thrust out of Egypt and could not tarry, neither had they made any provision for themselves"* (Ex. 12:39).

Today, *matzah* is striped and pierced for fast baking to ensure no leavening occurs.

On the Passover table, there are three special *matzot* wrapped in a white cloth. These have a very special meaning, which I will discuss under the heading of the Afikomen.

As is the custom with the wine, there is a traditional Hebrew blessing said for the bread: *Ba-ruch A-ta A-do-nai El-o-hei-nu, Melek Ha-olam, Ha-Motzi Le-chem min Ha-aretz* which means, "Blessed art Thou, O Lord our God, King of the universe, Who brings forth bread from the earth."

Interestingly, when Yeshua instituted the Communion, the blessings He said over the wine and the bread would have been exactly these two blessings.

Shankbone of a Lamb

The shankbone represents the Passover Lamb. On the afternoon of the night when the Angel of Death visited Egypt, the Israelites were told to kill a lamb without spot or blemish and sprinkle its blood on the door-posts and lintels over their door. When the Angel of Death saw the blood of the lamb, it passed by this house, and all who were inside were spared the horror of the death of the firstborn of that household. Those who did not do this suffered the loss of their firstborn. The promise was for all who obeyed the instructions given to Moses. Therefore, there may have been some God-fearing Egyptians who were spared if they too partici-pated. Likewise, if some Hebrews disregarded these instructions, then the Angel of Death was sure to have visited their homes. Believing and implementing God's Word into our lives carries with it the promise of blessing or cursing and should be taken very seriously.

Maror (Bitter Herbs)

The bitter herbs (usually horseradish) which are eaten, remind us of the bitter life and bondage in Egypt. For Christians, it can also remind us of the bitterness of sin.

The leader raises the bitter herbs and says, "This bitter herb which we eat, what does it mean? Because the Egyptians embittered the lives of our fathers in Egypt, as it is said, *'They embittered their lives with hard bondage, in mortar and brick, and with all work in the field. All their work was imposed upon them with rigor'"* (Ex. 1:14).

Today, there are many in the Church who seem to feel that it is per-missible to go back to "Egypt" (back into sin) occasionally. They feel they can somehow sin without reaping the bitterness. Here, during the meal, everyone has the opportunity to taste what "Egypt" is really like. Truly, you don't want to go back to Egypt.

Charoset

Symbolic Passover foods remind of various aspects of the Exodus from Egypt.

This is a sweet paste of chopped apples, nuts, raisins, cinnamon and sweet wine or grape juice. It is to remind us of the clay with which we once made bricks in Egypt. Its sweetness can also remind us that even while we made bricks in bondage, yet the Lord was with us. His pres-ence brought some sweetness into a difficult situation.

Karpas (Greens)

Parsley or celery is dipped into a small bowl of saltwater and eaten. This can remind us of several things: 1) the springtime when the Passover is celebrated, 2) the hyssop which was used to splash the blood of the Passover Lamb over the doorposts and lintels on the night of Israel's deliverance, and 3) the dipping of the greens in salt water gives us a taste of what it was like to cross the Red Sea with the people of Israel, who went in as a people and came out on the other side as a nation. It was a type of *mikvah*, or baptism. It can also give us a taste of the tears we shed when we lived in Egypt (or in sin).

The Roasted Egg

The egg is a later addition to the seder plate. Some say it is a reminder of the destruction of the Temple, as it replaces the shankbone of the lamb which is not present, since there is no sacrifice in the Temple today. Others say the egg represents the Jewish people, who despite severe persecution in exile, have survived as a people for 4,000 years. The egg is the only food that gets harder the more you cook it, just like the Jewish people around the world who have survived as a people, even under great pressures.

The Afikomen (Dessert)

I want us to look more closely at the *matzah*, the unleavened bread, which is striped and pierced to insure swift baking.

While there is plenty of **matzah** to eat during the meal, there is a ceremonial stack of three *matzot* which represent the following: 1) The top piece, God the Creator in Heaven, 2) The bottom piece, Humanity down on earth, and 3) The middle piece, the Mediating Priest.

At the beginning of the meal when the *matzah* is blessed, the middle piece (representing the mediating priest) is taken from the stack, blessed, broken, wrapped in a white cloth, and hidden away until after the meal. It is called the Afikomen, a Greek word literally meaning "dessert." The children of the house search for this hidden *matzah* after the meal. The elder of the house redeems it with a small gift or coin from the child who finds it. It is then blessed and eaten with the third cup of wine, the Cup of Redemption.

For the Christian, the Afikomen is a beautiful and strikingly clear picture of Yeshua. The *matzah* represents Messiah and His unleavened or sinless life. There was absolutely nothing in Him to puff Him up. On one occasion the Lord said, *"the Prince of this world comes, but he has nothing in Me"* (Jn. 14:30). Sin causes us to be *"puffed up"* (I Cor. 5:2). This is particularly obvious in sins such as pride, vanity, and vainglory. There was none of this in Yeshua.

The matzah is also striped and pierced. The Scripture says that *"with His stripes we are healed"* (Isa. 53:5), and we also know that Yeshua was pierced (Ps. 22:16; Isa. 53:15).

Just as the Afikomen, representing the mediating priest, is broken, wrapped in a white cloth and hidden away until after the meal, this reminds us of how our Lord, who is also the mediating priest, was also wrapped and hidden away in the tomb for three days after His death.

PASSOVER AND THE COMMUNION

For Christians, it is significant that it was this portion of bread, the Afikomen, that Yeshua blessed and gave to His disciples when instituting the new covenant sacrament of Communion. I believe this is why Yeshua said, *"I have eagerly desired to eat this passover with you before I suffer"* (Lk. 22:15).

We read in Matthew 26:26, that *"While they were eating, Yeshua took bread, gave thanks and broke it, and gave it to His disciples, saying, 'Take and eat; this is My body.'"*

Interestingly, it is also at this place in the seder meal when the third cup of wine, the Cup of Redemption, is blessed and drunk.

The third cup of the Passover is called the Cup of Redemption, for God says, *"I will redeem you with an outstretched arm"* (Ex. 6:6). We can now understand how this promise had a greater fulfillment when Yeshua was crucified. His arms were outstretched and nailed to the cross. His precious blood was shed for all mankind, so that through His sacrifice, we all can have forgiveness of sins and salvation. Then truly the Angel of Death will pass over our lives, because of the blood of the Lamb, Messiah Yeshua. John the Baptist said, *"Behold the Lamb of God who takes away the sin of the world"* (Jn. 1:29).

We read in Matthew 26:27-28 that Yeshua *"...took the cup, gave thanks and offered it to them, saying, 'Drink from it, all of you. This is My blood of the covenant, which is poured out for many for the forgiveness of sins.'"*

The Apostle Paul says of this bread and of this cup, *"For whenever you eat this bread and drink this cup, you proclaim the Lord's death until He comes"* (I Cor. 11:26).

It should be noted with interest, that Judas left the meal to go and betray Yeshua prior to the institution of the new covenant.

In accordance with the seder, the disciples and Yeshua sang a hymn and went out to the Garden of Gethse-mane where Yeshua was betrayed by Judas and arrested. Yeshua was tried, crucified, buried and resurrected.

We, as believers in Messiah Yeshua, can rejoice all the more, since as adopted sons of Abraham, we can commemorate not only the first

Passover and celebrate this festival of freedom, but we can also commemorate a second Passover, when Yeshua, the Lamb of God, gave Himself as a sacrifice for us, was buried and rose again, having conquered death so that we might have life everlasting in the Kingdom of God.

This celebration is what we do each time we take communion. But, in taking communion, how many of us really consider the fuller implications of the first Passover and what transpired during Passover week when Yeshua instituted the communion as a new covenant for us? For me, knowing this background makes the communion so much more meaningful.

THE FIRST CENTURY PASSOVER TABLE: WHERE DID THE DISCIPLES SIT AT THE LAST SUPPER?

You would not necessarily think it important to consider the table setting of the Last Supper or where the disciples sat. However, just the converse is true. If we understand this, it explains why certain things we read about in the Last Supper narratives were said and done.

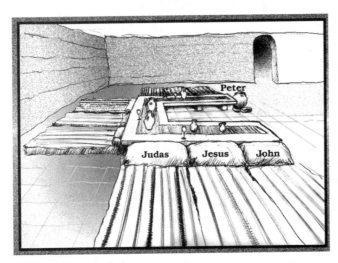

First, we need to consider the table setting itself. The Passover meal was a celebration of the Exodus and it was required to eat this meal in a manner usually reserved for the wealthy. That is to recline around the table, enjoying one's freedom in the Land. It would be impossible to recline around a table such as we eat at today. However, we do know that they ate around a U-shaped table, called a triclinium. It is placed low on the floor to allow for the people around it to recline on their left side while eating with their right hand. Everyone is facing the same direction around the table, often making it hard to speak to those behind you.

When looking at the triclinium, the left arm is the place of the most important guests, the cross arm is the place of the fairly important guests, and on the right arm we find the less important people, with the last seat on the end being called the Servant's Seat. If there were no servants present to serve the meal, then the person in the Servant's Seat had the job of waiting on those who had need of more food or drink.

At the triclinium table, the host (#2 seat, left arm of table) was protected from harm by his best friend seated at his right (#1 seat), while the seat of honor was to the host's left (#3 seat).

As with any table arrangement, certain seats had special functions, such as the last seat being the Servant's Seat. On the most important left arm, the second seat was that of the host. It was the custom that the first seat on the end was that of a trusted friend of the host. Why? This person helped protect the host, who might be a king or an important official. If someone tried to poison the host, the friend in seat #1, who would eat first, tested the food. Likewise, if someone charged into the room to throw a spear or dagger to kill the host, then the friend in seat #1 would be struck as his body protected the chest of the host. Seat #3 is the traditional seat of the most honored guest at the banquet. Therefore, the right and left hand of the host were considered important places. This is why John's mother made a request of Yeshua, *"Grant that one of these two sons of mine may sit at Your right and the other at Your left in Your kingdom"* (Mt. 20:21).

Reading the Gospel narratives and knowing what went on at the Last Supper, my friend and colleague, Dr. James Fleming of Biblical Resources, has speculated as to which disciples may have sat in which seats.

It is obvious that Yeshua was seated in seat #2, as He was the host. We also know that John was in seat #1, because John 13:23 tells us that John, *"the disciple whom Yeshua loved,"* was reclining next to Him. But, on which side? We know it was the right side because Peter motioned to John to ask Yeshua who was the one who would betray Him. The Bible tells us of John, *"Leaning back against Yeshua, he asked Him, 'Lord, who is it?'"* (Jn. 13:25). Around a triclinium, the only way to talk with the person behind you was to lean backwards. Since the custom was always to recline on your left side, that places John on the right of Yeshua.

So, who is seated in seat #3? It is speculated that this was the seat of Judas. When Yeshua responded to John's question as to who would be the betrayer, Yeshua said, *"He who has dipped his hand in the dish with Me, will betray Me"* (Mt. 26:23). Since everyone ate from common bowls, you would dip with people beside you. If John was on Yeshua's right hand, then obviously the only other candidate would be the person on Yeshua's left. But, why would Yeshua place Judas, of all people, in the seat of the most honored guest? Why not Peter, who was one of the inner circle and who had helped John prepare the room for the Passover? Perhaps it was Yeshua's way of saying to Judas, "I already know what you have done to betray Me, but I still want you to know that while I may hate your sin and betrayal, I still love you." This gesture of kindness must have deeply saddened Judas, the betrayer. His remorse at his betrayal of the One who loved him is probably why Judas went out and killed himself.

So, where is Peter? After all, he did help John prepare the triclinium room for the Passover, and he was one of the inner circle. Well, it is speculated that Peter was sitting in the last seat, the Servant's Seat. There are three good reasons to suggest this.

First, we know about Peter's impetuous personality. After he and John worked all day to prepare the room, when Yeshua and the disciples arrived, Peter surely thought he would be placed in one of the honored seats. Yeshua placed John to His right. But then, Peter was probably shocked to hear Yeshua ask Judas to sit at His left.

Impetuous Peter, feeling slighted, probably wanted to make a point. I can just hear Peter mumbling to himself, "I'll go sit in the lowliest seat, the Servant's Seat, and see what the Master will do. I remember Yeshua teaching us about humility and telling us: 'When we go to a banquet, don't sit in the high seats where you may be asked to move to a lowly seat and be dishonored. Rather, go sit in a lowly seat and wait to be asked to move up and thereby be honored!'" Stomping around the table to the last seat at the triclinium, Peter must have thought, "Surely, Yeshua will perceive my loyalty and devotion to Him and change my seat to a more honorable position nearer to Him." He then must have reclined in the last seat, looking uncomfortably at Yeshua with anticipation, hopeful that he would be moved. He was not moved.

There is a second indication that Peter was in this seat, because it would have been this person's job to carry around the basin and water to wash the hands of the guests. Whether this occurred or not is not recorded. However, Yeshua did something very unusual, with regard to washing, to make a point.

Always being the Teacher, Yeshua used this opportunity to teach His disciples about being a servant by His example. He got up and took the basin and towel and started to wash the feet of the disciples. Peter then realized his error in not washing everyone's hands in the beginning of the meal, and was grieved when he saw the Lord's selflessness when he was so selfish. We know that the last person Yeshua came to was Peter who immediately objected, because he was so humiliated by his error. The conversation in John 13:6-9 records their exchange:

Peter: *"Lord, are you going to wash my feet?"*

Yeshua replies: *"You do not yet realize now what I am doing, but later you will understand."*

Peter then declares, as His servant: *"No, you shall never wash my feet!"*

Yeshua, the Servant of all, answered: *"Unless I wash you, you have no part of Me."*

Peter responded: *"Then Lord, not just my feet, but my hands and my head, as well."*

How shocked and perplexed the disciples must have been to find the Teacher washing their feet! This was the Lord, and yet He was performing the most menial of tasks for them. Yeshua lived perfectly by the Law of the Torah, and was also able to challenge the traditions which had become lifeless. He breathed life upon the Commandments. Passover was yet another way given by the Lord for His followers to understand more about His character and who He really was.

Yeshua said to His disciples, *"Do you understand what I have done for you? You call me, 'Teacher' and 'Lord,' and rightly so, for that is what I am. Now that I, your Lord and Teacher, have washed your feet, you also should wash one another's feet. I have given you an example that you should do as I have done for you. I tell you the truth, no servant is greater than the one who sent him. Now that you know these things, you will be blessed if you do them"* (Jn. 13:12-17).

After this time of sharing great love and brotherhood between the disciples, Yeshua made the most profound revelation, *"Truly, I say to you, that one of you will betray Me"* (Mt. 26:21).

All the disciples became sad and began to say to Yeshua, *"Is it I, Lord?"* (Mt. 26: 22).

John records the third reason that we believe that Peter was seated in the Servant's Seat. John 13:24 says, *"Simon Peter motioned to [John] and said, 'Ask Him which one He means?"* Knowing that everyone reclines on their left side, John, being in seat #1, can see no one at the triclinium except the one directly across from him. I can just see the scene. Peter, already feeling humbled by his actions so far this evening, probably wondered if he were the one who was the betrayer. Anxious to know, he probably waved at or tossed an olive at John and urged him to ask the Lord directly. This is where John leans back into Yeshua and asks the question which revealed that Judas, in seat #3, was the betrayer.

Once revealed, Yeshua says to Judas, *"What you are about to do, do quickly"* (Jn. 13:27). Judas had left to betray the Master before the new covenant could be established.

I wish I had a video camera on Peter at this moment. Remember, seat #3 is the one he was wanting and made every effort to get. Now, he sees that that was the seat of the betrayer and he probably was happy to be as far away from him as he could get. So often in our walk with the Lord, we think what we want is best for us and get disappointed when God moves us in a different direction. Only later do we see that God's way is the best way and that our way is often selfish and self-serving. Maybe we all need to spend a little time in the "Servant's Seat" to learn that *"whosoever will be great among you, let him be your servant"* (Mt. 20:26b). In the Book of Acts, we see that Peter did become one of the greatest leaders of the early Church, full of the Lord and carrying His Gospel forth to the world.

OTHER LESSONS FROM THE PASSOVER AND THE FEASTS OF ISRAEL

The Last Supper was a Passover seder meal which Yeshua ate with His disciples. From this study into the Hebraic background, we have seen that there are deeper, spiritual meanings that we may not have realized before. Likewise, there were other New Testament events surrounding the festival of Passover and Pentecost, that take on new meaning when put into their Hebrew context.

For Passover, the people were required to present their lambs to the priest for inspection (on Nisan 10 on the Jewish calendar), four days before Passover. On this day, Yeshua, as the Lamb of God, presented Himself before the people and priests for inspection.

This event we know as Palm Sunday, when He rode into Jerusalem on a donkey to shouts of *"Hosanna! Save us!"* (Zech. 9:9). I Peter 1:18-19 says, *"Forasmuch as you know that you were not redeemed with corruptible things, like silver and gold, from your vain manner of life received by tradition from your fathers, but, with the precious blood of Christ, as of a lamb without blemish and without spot."*

Yeshua was betrayed and arrested on the Feast of Passover, Nisan 14 (Matt. 26:14-16). He was crucified with sinners, striped and pierced, wrapped in white linen and then buried over the Feast of Matzah, (unleavened bread), Nisan 15.

Then on the day after the first Sabbath of Passover, the prescribed day to celebrate the Feast of Firstfruits, Yeshua was resurrected, *"Messiah indeed has been raised from the dead, the firstfruit of those who have fallen asleep"* (I Cor. 15:20).

Fifty days later, on the Feast of Weeks (known as Shavuot or Pentecost), Israel celebrates the giving of the Law. It is also called the Water Holiday, and the Jewish children pour water on each other and anyone else whom they can, in celebration. During Pentecost, the Church received life and grace when God our Father sent His

Hosanna!

Spirit, the Water of Life, to all that believed in His Son, Yeshua. *"You will receive power when the Holy Spirit comes to you and you will be My witnesses in Jerusalem, and in all Judea and Samaria, and to the ends of the earth"* (Acts 1:8).

In Matthew 5:17, Yeshua says, *"Think not that I came to destroy the law and the prophets, I came not to destroy but to fulfill them."*

It was certainly not His intention that the Church would become as disconnected from our Hebraic roots as has happened. By reading and applying all of God's Word, we can understand more of the character of God and of Yeshua, and become better disciples.

As you celebrate Resurrection season, try to attend a Passover seder presentation and "experience" the first Passover. Also take the time to teach others about the background to the Passion week of Yeshua, and thereby "experience" a second Passover.

This Lesson from the Land of the Bible is found in our
Jerusalem Mosaic Video Series, Program #102,
along with other exciting features.
Please turn to page 186 to order your copy.

THE MEAL COVENANT

Chapter 7

Living in Israel, my two daughters, Ashley and Allison, love studying the Bible. We discuss the topics together and it really makes the Bible come alive for our entire family. This is especially true here in Israel where the street from our house to town gives us a glimpse of Bethlehem, the hills of Judea, and all of Jerusalem. We can stop almost anywhere, find that spot in the pages of the Bible and start talking about what God has done in this land, and what it means for us today.

Each spring, we enjoy Passover and Resurrection Sunday (Easter), celebrating each with a festive meal. Gathered together around the table with friends, it is a joyful time together with a certain feeling of "family." Over the meals we talk, have fellowship and strengthen our bonds of friendship. Being the teacher that I am, I can't have a gathering without discussing the mealtime dynamic that is going on around the table, because "breaking bread together" is actually very biblical.

*The **meal covenant** is a principle found throughout Scripture.*

Since you haven't been at the table with us, let me ask you the same questions I ask them:

- Why did Abraham and Melchizedek, Laban and Jacob eat a meal together?
- Why does Psalm 23 tell us that God *"prepares a table before us in the presence of our enemies?"*
- Why did the father of the prodigal son kill the fatted calf?
- Why did Yeshua (Jesus) institute the sacrament of Communion at the Passover meal/Last Supper?
- Why did Yeshua (Jesus) prepare a meal on the shore of the Sea of Galilee for Peter and then tell Peter, *"Feed My sheep?"*
- In Revelation 3:20, why does Yeshua want us to open the door so He can come in and eat with us?

Notice that each event was related to a meal. Now even if you know some of the answers to these questions, allow me to share with you what I share around our holiday table in hopes that it will give you some new insights into God's Word.

The thread that ties the above questions together is the Meal Covenant or the Covenant of Reconciliation. Now, don't start looking up this covenant in your Bible concordance, because you won't find it mentioned. The Meal Covenant is not prescribed in the Bible like the regulations given for Temple worship or the practices required for celebrating the feasts. Rather, the meal covenant is a principle found throughout Scripture, whereby a meal becomes the means for reconciliation between people. Even God uses the meal to remind people of His relationship to us and our need for reconciliation to HIM.

Let's look together at a few examples from Scripture to answer the questions.

ABRAM AND MELCHIZEDEK

We first see the meal covenant expressed in Genesis 14 after Abram killed Kedorlaomer, King of Elam, who had taken his nephew Lot captive. Melchizedek, king of Salem (Jerusalem) and Priest of the Most High God, met Abram and blessed him, bringing "bread and wine" for them to eat together as a sign of a covenant being established between the two men.

JACOB AND LABAN

The next time we see the meal as a sign of reconciliation is in Genesis 31, when Jacob took Leah and Rachel, his children and cattle, and left his father-in-law, Laban, to go back to Bethel. He left in secret and without letting Laban say goodbye to his family. Laban followed him across the desert in desperation and anger. When he caught up with Jacob, they had a long talk and were reconciled to one another. They set up a mound of rocks and a stone for a pillar, promising that neither would come after the other to harm each other (Gen. 31:52).

Then, he (Jacob) offered a sacrifice and invited his relatives to a meal. After they had eaten, they spent the night there. Early the next morning Laban kissed his grandchildren and his daughters and blessed them. Then he left and returned home (Gen. 31:54-55). It is a rather lengthy story, and the entire process of family reconciliation was ultimately sealed with a meal.

PSALM 23

In Psalms 23:5,6, it says of God, *"You prepare a table before me in the presence of my enemies. Surely goodness and mercy will follow me all the days of my life, and I will dwell in the house of the LORD forever."* When

I first became a born-again Christian, Psalm 23 was one of the first passages of Scripture I memorized. I was rather young and could not imagine what it meant to have a table set in the presence of my enemies. I honestly pictured David on an ancient, biblical battlefield, reclining without fear, next to a picnic blanket spread with a meal, as the enemy shot arrows and threw spears over his head.

Abraham and his people lived a nomadic life. They probably lived in tents similar to the Bedouin ones shown here. Today, Bedouin tents can still be seen in Israel.

Seriously, unless you understand the concept of reconciliation associated with a meal, this verse does not make much sense. In Hebraic symbolism, God's setting a table before your enemies means that He is making the way possible for you to be "reconciled" to your enemies. That is why your cup overflows (the Hebraic symbol of joy), and you realize that surely goodness and mercy will follow you all the days of your life *"as you dwell in the house of the Lord forever."* It can be your assurance that God will take care of you and can even deal with your enemies, even providing for reconciliation.

Today, between the Bedouin tribes and in the Arab village communities in the Middle East, we find the practice of the "sulha," or reconciliation meal, between enemies. Interestingly, this Arabic term, "sulha," comes from the Hebrew word for table, "shulchan." Periodically, you can read in the Israeli newspapers that a "sulha" is being made between rival groups or families where a feud has existed, with the purpose of ending the feud once and for all.

How does it work? Let's say that a young man seriously injuries another young man from a different family. You can imagine that there would be a major blood feud, especially in a small, close-knit community where everyone knows everyone. If the feud gets out of hand, there could be more injury and even death. The only way to stop it is to resolve the conflict and reconcile the families. That is the purpose of the "sulha."

A big meal is prepared and the two factions come together to eat. The guilty party confesses his wrongdoing and the injured party accepts the confession. They then negotiate a suitable recompense for the misdeed. This negotiation may go on for a day or more, until everyone is satisfied.

All this time, the parties are "at table," eating and drinking coffee and tea. At the conclusion of the "sulha" negotiation, the two parties and families are fully reconciled, and a member of the injured family cannot later bring up the misdeed to the offender or to his family. It becomes almost as if it never happened.

What a wonderful picture of how God justifies our sin by the sacrifice of Yeshua on the cross, symbolized in the Communion. As Christians, our sin is literally erased before the Lord and we can stand before Him, spotless.

THE PRODIGAL SON

In Luke 15:11-31, we find the parable of the lost son, more commonly known as the story of "the Prodigal Son," which contains my favorite example of the meal covenant.

Let's read this story together and then we can interpret its fuller meaning:

"There was a man who had two sons. The younger one said to his father, 'Father, give me my share of the estate.' So he divided his property between them. Not long after that, the younger son got together all he had, set off for a distant country and there squandered his wealth in wild living. After he had spent everything, there was a severe famine in that whole country, and he began to be in need. So he went and hired himself out to a citizen of that country, who sent him to his fields to feed pigs."

It is presumed that the younger son found himself in the Decapolis, an area of Greek hegemony and culture which encompassed the southeastern shores of the Sea of Galilee. The Jews of Israel would not raise pigs, as this was not kosher, but Greeks would. Incidentally, this is also the location of the town of Kursi, where Yeshua cast the legion of demons into a herd of swine, which threw themselves into the sea and drowned. Let's continue with verse 16:

"I have sinned against heaven and against you. I am no longer worthy to be called your son; make me like one of your hired men."

"He longed to fill his stomach with the pods that the pigs were eating, but no one gave him anything. When he came to his senses, he said, 'How many of my father's hired men have food to spare, and here I am starving to death! I will set out and go back to my father and say to him: Father, I have sinned against heaven and against you. I am no longer worthy to be called your son; make me like one of your hired men.'

"So he got up and went to his father. But while he was still a long way off, his father saw him and was filled with compassion for him; he ran to his son, threw his arms around him and kissed him. The son said to him,

'Father, I have sinned against heaven and against you. I am no longer worthy to be called your son.' But the father said to his servants, -'Quick! Bring the best robe and put it on him. Put a ring on his finger and sandals on his feet. Bring the fatted calf and kill it. Let's have a feast and celebrate. For this son of mine was dead and is alive again; he was lost and is found.' So they began to celebrate."

The younger son was humbled by the experience. On his way home he composed his 4-point sermon confessing his sin against God in heaven and his father. He was only going to ask to be reinstated as one of his father's servants, not as a son. However, upon hearing his son's confession, his father reinstated him as his son not by word, but by deeds. By doing four things the father showed everyone that this was his son returned home, and not one of his servants. What did the father do?

He gave his younger son a robe and sandals, both signs of sonship, not servanthood. Servants wore tunics and did not have the outer garments, nor did they have sandals. These were reserved for the sons of a household.

The father also gave him his ring, which was the "credit card" of the day. With the ring, the son could go to town, and receive credit to buy merchandise by simply pressing the family ring into the soft clay. His father would later pay the bill.

Think about this - even after what the younger son did by abusing his finances, his father was still, STILL willing to trust him. This is also a picture of what God does for us after we confess our wrongdoings and receive His forgiveness.

Finally, the father killed a fatted calf for a celebration banquet. This was more than a dinner party, but a sure sign of absolute reconciliation to be witnessed by the whole community in attendance.

This is my favorite example because it shows us God's character for complete restoration. And, it is also an example of how we should act towards others. The father demonstrated and tangibly backed up his words with his actions as he restored his son's position with the clothing of a son, trust with the "credit card," and finally by preparing the banquet meal of reconciliation. Often, we have good intentions towards others and our words are even noble, but sometimes our actions fall short of the mark.

Now let's see what happened to the older brother beginning with verse 25: *"Meanwhile, the older son was in the field. When he came near the house, he heard music and dancing. So he called one of the servants and asked him what was going on. 'Your brother has come,' he replied, 'and your father has killed the fatted calf because he has him back safe and sound.'*

"The older brother became angry and refused to go in. So his father went out and pleaded with him. But he answered his father, 'Look! All these years I've been slaving for you and never disobeyed your orders. Yet you never gave me even a young goat so I could celebrate with my friends. But when this son of yours who has squandered your property with prostitutes comes home, you kill the fatted calf for him!' 'My son,' the father said, 'you are always with me, and everything I have is yours.'"

The older brother is the picture of ourselves and how we often fall short in our ability to forgive. It seems natural for the older brother to have been angry. After all, he worked faithfully for his father, and now sees what is going on. His younger brother, who had squandered his inheritance, was being treated with dignity and was being celebrated with a banquet that included a fatted calf!

When I first read this passage and I did not understand the meaning of this symbol. I sided with the angry older brother who never received even a goat to have a banquet with his friends. However, the father, who understood the meaning of preparing the special reconciliation meal before the whole neighborhood, knew that there was no reason to "kill the fatted calf" for his older son. There was no need to reconcile him back to the family and to the community. The older son already had it all! That is why the father said to his older son, *"My son, you are always with me, and EVERYTHING I have is yours."*

Yet, the older brother lost the blessing by not going to the banquet. He is not mentioned again and he apparently left the party in misery, remaining outside of the circle of the reunion and reconciliation with his brother.

Are we sometimes like the older brother? Are we, who have received ALL from the Lord, often unwilling or unable to come to the place of forgiveness and reconciliation towards others who we feel have wronged us? Sadly, like the older brother, if we continue in our bitterness and anger, we will not be able to join in the fullness of God's celebration, which forgiveness and reconciliation always provide. Let us learn from this lesson and NOT repeat it.

FEED MY LAMBS (SHEEP)

Jesus eating a meal of reconciliation with Peter.

In John 21:12, we find the resurrected Yeshua inviting the disciples to a breakfast of fish and bread on the shores of the Sea of Galilee.

Peter had denied Yeshua three times in Jerusalem. Peter was humiliated and had given up and gone back to his old fishing job, in the Galilee. And then there was Yeshua on the shore, just like the first time Peter met Him. Peter hears the same miraculous message to throw his net to the other side of the boat for a great catch of fish. Peter catches the fish and then realizes it really is Yeshua. Peter jumps into the water. He doesn't walk on the water this time, but falls in. He gets to the shore and they begin to eat. Ghosts don't eat fish; resurrected bodies do.

Yeshua knew Peter had denied him three times back in Jerusalem and His purpose was to reinstate Peter over a meal on the beach. Peter is eating with Yeshua, when Yeshua asks Peter three times, "Peter, do you love me?" And each time when Peter says, "Yes," Yeshua instructs him, "Feed My lambs." By asking Peter three times if Peter loved Him, Yeshua reminded Peter of his three denials. He then confirmed to Peter that his calling was to feed the lambs of Yeshua. In other words, Peter was to reconcile wayward lambs back to the Kingdom of God, just as Yeshua had done for him.

There is a double reconciliation in this passage: First, Peter was restored to fellowship with Yeshua, whom he had denied. Then, Peter is called to do the same for others who have gone astray.

"I STAND AT THE DOOR AND KNOCK"

In Revelation 3:20 we find Yeshua saying, *"Here I am! I stand at the door and knock. If anyone hears My voice and opens the door, I will come in and eat with him, and he with Me."*

For Christians, this bring us back to Communion, at the Passover - Last Supper table, to the same bread and wine brought forth by Melchizedek, the High Priest of the Most High God back in Genesis. It can also remind us of the future marriage feast of the Lamb, as the Bridegroom comes for His bride!

The communion table is the table of reconciliation. The purpose of communion is to remind us of what Yeshua did so that we can appropriate that event, as we receive God's forgiveness, reconciling us to the Lord.

Yes, Yeshua, the sinless one, the one without leaven, the Passover lamb without spot or blemish, was crucified and died for our sins, so that as Christians, we might have eternal life and a restored relationship with God. At Passover, Yeshua was crucified, wrapped in white linen and buried. But, He rose on the third day, the firstfruits of many. In Revelation 3:20, He is now the resurrected God, making the way for sinful man to hear His voice, to open their heart's door, letting him in to sup.

The symbol of the table of reconciliation is the same one expressed throughout Scripture. Yet, this time the intention is eternal reconciliation. And even after we attain so great a salvation, it is at the communion table, when Christians eat the bread and drink the wine, that the covenant is reconfirmed in our lives.

What does this mean for you and me? Temporally, we need to realize that something dynamic takes place between people at mealtime while "breaking bread together," where there is time to fellowship, resolve problems and establish strong family and friendship bonds. What do you think is happening to these bonds in our fast-paced, instant, microwave-world where the family meal is often a lost art? How can we maintain strong relationships "on the run," always grabbing a bite of food in the "drive-thru window" of fast-food establishments? Please, get back to the family meal and take time to eat with friends. You won't regret it.

Spiritually, God is a God of mercy and reconciliation. He is there for each one of us, no matter what is in our past. God desires our fellowship and has made the way for our reconciliation to Him. As a Christian, even if you have gone your own way as a prodigal son or daughter, you can come back to Him and be reconciled to Him. It is always His desire. In His love, He wants to bring each of us back into fellowship with Him. Then, when a "brother" needs forgiving, do so and back it up with actions, in the same way that God forgives us. Get right with God and get right with others. Do it today!

This Lesson from the Land of the Bible is found in our
Jerusalem Mosaic Video Series, Program #108,
along with other exciting features.
Please turn to page 186 to order your copy.

LESSONS FROM SUKKOT

THE FEAST OF TABERNACLES

Chapter 8

AWESOME! Young people in most English-speaking countries currently use this word to describe an amazing or incredible action or event. Webster defines "awesome" as "full of, or inspiring awe" which is "a mixed feeling of reverence, fear, and wonder." The three times it appears in the King James Bible it describes the sense of the presence of God which inspires a human response of fear or awe.

Only God - and His acts - can truly be described as awesome. When we contemplate the mighty works of God, our Father in heaven, the King of Kings and Lord of Lords, we enter into the realm of the awesome.

Our awesome God is known by many names and characteristics:

- *El Shaddai*, the All Sufficient One
- *Yahweh Shammah*, the Lord is There
- *Yahweh Mekoddeshkem*, the Lord Sanctifies You
- *Yahweh Tsidkenu*, the Lord Our Righteousness
- *Elohim, God*, Mighty and Strong, the Creator
- A God who is so powerful that if we looked upon His face we would be consumed, yet so gentle and loving that He counts the hairs on our heads and knows when even a sparrow falls.
- A God who so desired fellowship with us, that when His creation fell to sin, He provided the means for forgiveness of that sin so that we could enjoy citizenship in the Kingdom of God.

If we allow our minds to dwell on these things we will experience awe - a feeling of reverence mixed with fear and wonder. We will also be reminded of related concepts, such as:

- God's SOVEREIGNTY, His supremacy. He is above all others in power and rank.
- God's MAJESTY, a word connoting grandeur and dignity or a term used when speaking to or of a sovereign,
- God's AUTHORITY, the power or right to give commands and take action.

The four species used during Sukkot.

83

We often forget these attributes of God in the midst of our trials and tribulations. We often grumble or crumble under the weight of the circumstances. Sometimes we are so filled with our own self-importance and self-sufficiency that we forget the awesomeness of God. We think we can handle our own lives and thereby prove the truth of the verse, *"Pride goes before destruction and a haughty spirit before a fall" (Prov. 16:18)*. And, fall we do.

When we forget the omniscience, omnipresence, and omnipotence (that's the all-knowing, everywhere present, and all-powerful character) of God, our lives fall into disarray and get out of order. We backslide - not only from God, but from others. Edmund Burke said, "Whatever disunites man from God disunites man from man." So, what's the solution? We all need be aware of our position as "creations" under the authority of the Creator, to keep our lives *b'seder* - Hebrew for *in order.* We need to be reminded of God in all His glory and splendor and of what He has done for us, so we can rightly assess our place in His plan. The biblical festival of *Sukkot* (Tabernacles) provides such a time of remembrance.

SUKKOT: A REMINDER OF GOD'S MAJESTY

Each of the biblical Jewish holidays teaches us something unique and wonderful about our relationship with God, our creator, sustainer and provider. Without Him we are ruined - spiritually and even physically. The holidays teach various lessons: God has saved us (*Pesach* - Passover), provided for us (*Shavuot* - Firstfruits) and *Sukkot* - Tabernacles), called us (*Rosh Hashana* - Trumpets), redeemed us (*Yom Kippur* - Atonement), and provided guidance for us by His Word (*Simchat Torah* - the Joy of God's Word). Living in Israel, I am privileged to participate in a society that keeps *Sukkot*. The symbols of *Sukkot* always bring me into the presence of God in a new way. Confronted with God's sovereignty, I am always aware of my own frailty and need of Him.

WHAT IS SUKKOT?

The biblical description of this festival can be found in several places. The most prominent are: Leviticus 23:34-43, Deuteronomy 16:13-15, and Numbers 29:12-40. Take time to read these passages.

Tabernacles is a week-long autumn harvest festival. It occurs in the Hebrew month of Tishri, September or October each year. There are two main elements to the holiday:

1. The building of booths (called *Sukkot*, in Hebrew).
2. The sacrifices.

Each provides important lessons for us.

The holiday commemorates the desert wanderings of the Children of Israel, when they came out of Egypt on their way to the Promised Land. Even though they were wandering because of their own disobedience, God was with them and divinely protected them and provided for their needs.

For the celebration of *Sukkot*, the Israelites were commanded to build tabernacles or booths and actually live in them for a week each year, so they could remember God's presence and His faithfulness as a protector and provider.

The Festival of *Sukkot*, one of the seven Levitical feasts, seems to be the only major biblical festival which has no direct fulfillment or parallel in the New Testament. While the other major Biblical festivals have a large degree of fulfillment, this festival remains a festival of the future, shrouded in symbolism and mystery (Zech. 14:16). The fact that many Christians have developed an interest in the celebration of *Sukkot* may indicate the significance of the prophetic times in which we live.

A TIME OF JOY

God commands Sukkot to be a season of joy and rejoicing. All the festivals, including Shabbat, are times when troubles are left behind because it is forbidden to bear a burden on a festival day (Lev. 23:35).

Men carry the traditional lulav and citron to the synagogue to wave as they rejoice before the Lord, as commanded by the Lord in Leviticus 23:40. The lulav has three branches tied together: a palm frond, a willow branch, and a myrtle branch. The citron is a citrus fruit that smells like a lemon.

Jewish tradition provides us with a practical understanding of a truly spiritual life based on the characteristics of the lulav and citron.

• Spiritually, we are not to be like the **PALM**, as it can only bear fruit (deeds), but is not fragrant (spiritual blessing). We have all met folks who live their lives by the letter of the law but have no love or compassion in administering it, for themselves or others.

• We are not to be like the **MYR-TLE**, as it only has fragrance, but can't bear fruit. We have met those who are "so heavenly minded they are no earthly good." They may say spiritual things and may be very sweet people, but their lives don't produce any real lasting fruit.

• We are not to be like the **WILLOW**, as it can neither produce fruit nor fragrance. This speaks of people who are blown around by every wind of doctrine and never quite know where they are spiritually. Therefore, they produce no fruit.

• We are to be like the **CITRON**, which produces both fruit and fragrance. These are God's steadfast believers who live a balanced life in wisdom before God and man.

We should strive to be like the citron.

THE SUKKAH (BOOTH)

As you look in the yards and on the balconies in Jerusalem, you can see all kinds of *sukkot* or booths built for families to dwell in for the week of the holiday. The *sukkah* is a temporary structure. Traditionally, the building begins on the night Yom Kippur is over, which is four days before *Sukkot* begins.

The *sukkah* is four-sided with an opening on one side. Almost any building material will do for the sides, so long as it is not of a permanent nature. The top is loosely covered with branches from "goodly trees," taking care you are able to see an occasional star. The *sukkah* is usually decorated with fruit dangling on strings from the roof, since *Sukkot* is the harvest festival of God's provision, which also signifies the ingathering of all the fruit of the earth (Lev. 23:39). It is thus a festival of the end-times. The children also like to add tinsel, streamers, paper-chains, and pictures depicting Bible stories. (For a complete description of how to build a *sukkah*, please see the instructions at the end of the chapter.)

Meals are eaten in the *sukkah,* accompanied by singing and rejoicing. Some very observant families like to spend leisure time and even sleep there. It is also a place to discuss and meditate on the lessons from this flimsy dwelling of Israel's past. Spending time in your booth is a reminder that God brought the Children of Israel out of the bondage of their Egyptian taskmasters into freedom. As Christians, we can celebrate that God redeemed us from a life of bondage to sin and brought us into His freedom in the Kingdom of God. This is a joyful celebration.

Each year my family and I join in this festival and build our booth on an outdoor porch. Ashley and Allison, our girls, really look forward to the preparation and decoration. Each night for a week we eat our meals there and retell the story of how God provided for the Children of Israel in the desert and discuss how He provides for us. We sing songs of praise to the Lord, just as our neighbors do. We can feel the night breeze as it rustles through the leaves, occasionally catching the twinkle of the stars above our branches. Each year we learn and understand more about our Lord and His ways.

This exercise is much more than a cultural or historical exchange. It is a biblical experience that can teach us new insights about the Lord as we do it.

WHAT ARE SOME OF THE LESSONS WE CAN LEARN FROM THE SUKKAH?

LESSON #1: WE ARE ALL SOJOURNERS

From the days of our father Abraham, we have been strangers and pilgrims in the earth. God seems to desire it this way.

It has also spelled disaster when God's people grew too comfortable. This was undoubtedly one of the reasons why God issued the command for the Israelites to dwell in booths for one week each year, and why the custom is to be continued as a *"statute forever"* (Lev. 23:41).

As **SOJOURNERS** (I Pt. 2:11), we must learn to hold all things loosely. This is especially difficult in our materialistic age. We are constantly held by the tyranny of "things." Things control and manipulate us; they become gods, or idols, over us. As the people of Israel were about to enter the land, God impressed upon them the message of Tabernacles, lest they be drawn away by the very affluence of the Promised Land. The message is still a good one today.

When the Israelites were wanderers in the desert they all lived in tents.

Christians also must learn that this life is only temporary. We, too, are on a pilgrimage to a Promised Land in eternity. We need to seek God's kingdom, not earthly comfort. As we seek first the kingdom of God, our material needs are provided for by the Lord (Lk. 12:31).

Finally, sojourning is a great **EQUALIZER.** When the Israelites were wanderers in the desert they all lived in tents - rich and poor alike. The book of Deuteronomy speaks of all the people going to their *tents.* After the children of Israel entered the Promised Land, the book of Judges mentions *tents and houses.* By the time of the books of Kings, the author speaks of *tents, houses and palaces.* During Tabernacles, all men are equal before God and one another. Each one sits in his flimsy *sukkah* and considers God, not his own special status.

Most of us have been sojourners as we traveled on vacation or business trips. Certainly those of you who have joined us on Israel tours know that when you are with a group of people, everyone is vulnerable to circumstances beyond their own control. Everyone in the group travels with only their basic needs. They are not in their usual "societal roles" that might intimidate others. Traveling as a group brings down barriers. Instant conversation and newfound friendships are possible with people you might have been too intimidated to talk with in your home community. During *Sukkot*, temporarily "sojourning" in your *sukkah* gives you an annual opportunity to reflect on how you relate to God and to others.

LESSON #2: OUR FAITH REQUIRES FLEXIBILITY

We must be able to move when God moves. Christian history is filled with those who had vested interests that prevented them from moving when God moved. The tabernacle is a flimsy structure. It is almost a tent and can be put up or taken down in a few minutes. It is sensitive to the wind of the Holy Spirit. It is open to the heavens; it is indefensible and cannot be closed off.

Throughout the Bible, it seems that the struggle has gone on between the concept of tabernacle *(sukkah* or *mishkan)* and the concept of house *(bayit)*. The whole episode of Stephen's stoning seemed to revolve around this issue. Stephen told his hearers that David *"desired to find a tabernacle for the God of Jacob, but Solomon built Him a house"* (Acts 7:46-47).

Certainly, the house is a more attractive, more comfortable, more durable and appealing human habitation. Yet in the house, we lose the flexibility to follow the cloud, we lose the sensitivity to the wind and we lose that intimate contact with the creation and the Creator.

The Bible looks forward to a time of purer and simpler faith. The prophet Amos speaks of the end days as a time when the Tabernacle of David will be restored (Amos 9:11). That flimsy tent with its glorious worship and fellowship with God has probably touched both Judaism and Christianity more than any of us realize. David's worship, his Psalms and his ecstasy before God, has surely influenced many outbreaks of revival in both Jewish and Christian history. It is noteworthy that some of the great revivals actually were held in tents and brush arbors, closely resembling the ancient tabernacle.

With this in mind we can better understand the movement of the last days spoken of by John in Revelation: "Behold, the tabernacle of God is with men, and He will dwell with them, and they shall be His people, and God Himself shall be with them, and be their God" (Rev. 21:3).

The tabernacle may have been a fragile and unsightly structure, but it enabled the Israelites to look out the tent door and see the glory of God hovering over them in the pillar of cloud and fire. Throughout subsequent history, both Israel and the Church have traded away spiritual reality for human security.

LESSON #3: WE MUST REMEMBER THE FRAILTY OF OUR OWN LIVES

As you sit in the *sukkah* and watch the wind rustle the leaves overhead, some will fall around you. Early in the week of *Sukkot*, the leaves are fresh and green, but soon they are dry and dead. The verse of Isaiah 64:6

becomes especially clear, *"We all do fade as a leaf, and our iniquities like the wind, have taken us away."*

With the "house" concept it is easy for us to feel permanent and self-sufficient and to lose sight of our very brief sojourn on the earth. As the flight attendant announces on a short stopover, "Our ground time here will be brief." The tabernacle also speaks of our frailty, that we are but flesh. Yet in our frailty, we are reminded that God provides (Jehovah Jireh), for which we should be thankful. However, the very consistency of God's provision and blessing sometimes dulls our gratitude. The greatest thing about God's blessings is that they are fresh each day (Lam. 3:23). They are new every morning - Great is His faithfulness. We didn't do it ourselves.

The New Testament writers often refer to our bodies as a tabernacle (II Pet. 1:13). Paul reminds us that *"... if the earthly tent we live in is destroyed, we have a building from God, an eternal house in heaven"* (II Cor. 5:1).

Like the Tabernacle, we too are flimsy and frail, and soon begin to fade. Life is short. Our hope is not in what the world has to offer, but in what God has already provided for us to serve Him here and now, and for eternity. Yeshua (Jesus) said, *"In My Father's house are many mansions — I am going to prepare a place for you. And if I go and prepare a place for you, I will come back and take you to be with Me that you also may be where I am "*(Jn. 14:2,3). The place for our permanent "house" abode is in eternity.

THE SACRIFICE

The second main element of *Sukkot,* one that is hardly ever mentioned, is the admonition to sacrifice, found in Leviticus 23:37-39 and more fully described in Numbers 29:12-20. The Israelites were supposed to bring burnt offerings, grain offerings, sacrifices and drink offerings EACH DAY of the week of Sukkot! This was costly and time-consuming.

Imagine if we had to fulfill these daily requirements? Would we do it? Do we have that much commitment to the Lord? Would we be willing to sustain the cost of these rich sacrifices or would we find an excuse to avoid participating? If it is so hard, then why did God require the sacrifices?

The underlying purpose of the offerings was to be purified from sin so that the worshipper could enter into fellowship with God. The requirements were stiff. The basic principle is obedience. God provided for the sacrifice, but were His people faithful to lay it on the altar? That took faith.

Without obedience and faith, the offerings were valueless. It was not enough to go through the motions of making a sacrifice, if there was no repentance and a subsequent effort to live a Godly life each day. We can forget the sacrifice if we are not willing to be obedient and faithful.

FAITH WITHOUT WORKS IS DEAD

Likewise for Christians, without faith and practice, the sacrificial, atoning death of the Lamb of God is valueless. It is not enough to know the facts of the story. If we don't appropriate it personally and act upon it by faith, then we will not have the promised salvation. It is God's gift, but we have to receive it and then live it. *"For by grace we are saved through faith. It is a gift of God, not of works, lest any man should boast"* (Eph. 2:8,9). Yet James 2:17 tells us that, *"Faith without works is dead, being alone."*

This is not a contradiction, but a qualification. If our faith does not yield fruit through works of faith, then the faith is not true faith, and it is dead. It is the obedience of acting on our faith, even sacrificially, that proves it to be true.

TO SACRIFICE IS TO GIVE, NOT JUST GET

Another lesson of the sacrifice focuses our attention on what we can, and should, give to the Lord. Too often in our late, 20th century evangelical Christianity, particularly in some of the North American groups, the emphasis is on what we can "get" from the Lord, and not on what we should be giving. Certainly, we are blessed by the Lord as we are faithful to give. Yet, the blessing should be the fringe benefit, not the sole motivation for giving.

Sukkot reminds us of God's sovereignty and majesty. It also reminds us of the need to honor Him with our lives and give back to God from the provisions and blessings He has given to us. The tithe is a requirement of God (Mal. 3:10) that even predates the Law (Gen. 14:20; 28:22).

For Christians, Romans 12:1 asks more of us than a grain or drink offering. God requires our lives. *"Therefore, I urge you, brothers, in view of God's mercy, to offer your bodies as living sacrifices, holy and pleasing to God - which is your spiritual worship."*

We have so much to give to the Lord:
- God gave us our lives, so we can give them back to Him in service.
- God sustains us with income, food, clothing, and shelter, which we can give to His service.
- God gives us each talents, which we can lay before the throne of God for His service.
- God gives us our salvation and love to share this message with others.
- God gives us the fruit of His Spirit: love, joy, peace, patience, gentleness, goodness, faith, meekness, and self-control (Gal. 5:22).

GOD'S BLESSING, OUR RESPONSE

We need to be producing spiritual fruit and fragrance and by this be storing up our treasures in heaven where moth and rust do not corrupt. Treasures in heaven are laid up only as treasures on earth are laid down.

Sukkot is more than just sitting under the decorative fruits of His creation. It is to consider that we are His creation. We are to gather up our personal, spiritual fruits of faith and celebrate by giving ourselves in God's service.

In 1961 John F. Kennedy said in his inauguration speech as President of the US, "Ask not what your country can do for you, ask what you can do for your country." Today, we can ask ourselves, "Ask not what our God can do for you, ask what you can do for our God." The message of Sukkot is total commitment to the Lord and His service.

The final holiday of the fall festival cycle is SIMCHAT TORAH, meaning, "celebrating the joy of God's Word." This holiday is the day following Sukkot when the people finish the annual Torah reading cycle with Deuteronomy 34 and begin it again by reading Genesis 1. There is great celebration because it is the Word of God that provides us with life's instruction book for righteous and abundant living. In Israel, the neighborhood streets are filled with people as whole congregations pour out of the synagogues carrying their Torah scrolls high in the air as they sing and chant in celebration. Can you imagine the effect on the neighborhood if your congregation did the same thing with your Bibles raised in the air? People would ask a lot of questions, and you could share with them the joy of serving the Lord God of Israel.

Are we ready to put our lives on the line for God? He is inviting us to a celebration. Let's start today.

If you want to know how to build a sukkah in your backyard, we have included some simple instructions to help you get started.

TRY BUILDING YOUR OWN SUKKAH

It is considered to be a *mitzvah* (good deed) to build your own *sukkah*. Actually it is not such a difficult job. You will need to start planning early though, in order to begin your construction as quickly as possible after Yom Kippur, the Day of Atonement. Here in Israel some devout Jews begin construction as soon as the sun is down on Yom Kippur, four days before *Sukkot* starts.

Since the *sukkah* is not to be an elaborate or permanent structure, the

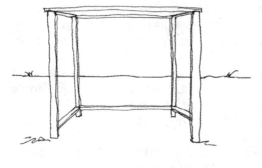

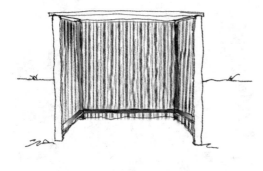

most inexpensive materials may be used. You will need 4 light-weight posts (2 x 2s in the U.S.) for the corners, 4 more poles (2 x 2s) for the roof. All should be approximately 7 or 8 feet (2.5 meters) in length. To cover the roof you will need several slats or small boards capable of holding up light tree branches. For the sides, old bedsheets seem to work well. Other materials like canvas, cane matting, heavy cardboard, or light plywood are also fine. You will need enough to enclose three sides, with a drape for the entrance. For the top you simply need to trim a few trees in the back yard.

Now for the actual construction. The tabernacle can be almost any size so long as it is large enough to sit in. We are recommending a seven foot cube (2.5 meters), since this will allow plenty of room for guests.

The sukkah is meant to be a temporary structure, so all materials are lightweight and easy to handle, or repair should a strong wind arise.

Nail four poles together to form a square. Then tack a post to each corner, and have a friend help you set your sukkah upright. If you wish, you may anchor the uprights in the holes of stacked concrete blocks or bricks. You may also use an existing building for one side of your sukkah. Once your sukkah frame has been set up, drape bed sheets or other coverings around three sides. In the front, a bed sheet attached on a wire track works well for a door. Finally, place the tree branches on top, but not so thick as to obscure the stars shining through.

The *sukkah* can now be outfitted to your own taste. Many people furnish their *sukkah* with a table and chairs. You may wish to decorate the walls with pictures or Bible verses. Fruit should be hung from the ceiling; paper chains and other decorations may be hung on the walls. Use your imagination, and by all means, let the children participate.

All that is left now is the enjoyment. Invite your friends to see your masterpiece and rejoice with you. Try a meal out in the *sukkah*, or even spend the night there. It will be an unforgettable and blessed experience.

This Lesson from the Land of the Bible is found in our
Jerusalem Mosaic Video Series, Program #111,
along with other exciting features.
Please turn to page 186 to order your copy.

Part II

The Land of Israel
and
Prophecy

"I will bring back my exiled people Israel;
they will rebuild the ruined cities and live in
them. They will plant vineyards
and drink their wine; they will make
gardens and eat their fruit. I will plant Israel
in their own land, never again
to be uprooted from the land I have given them"
(Amos 9:14-15).

The Land of Israel and Prophecy

God chose Israel and the Jewish people to be His instruments on earth to bring salvation to the world. God never had a Plan A for the Jewish people and a Plan B for the Gentile Church. He has only had a Plan A, and we as a Church were brought into God's ongoing redemptive process that is still connected to the Land of Israel, which God calls His own. The world and spiritual forces have fought God's plans throughout the ages.

Nearly 2,000 years ago, the enemies of Israel attempted to overthrow and erase God's covenantal relationship between Israel and the Jewish people. In two wars between the Jews and Rome in 70 and 135 AD, the Romans destroyed the Temple of God; exiled most of the Jewish people from the Land of Israel; changed Israel's name to Palestine, reminiscent of the arch-enemies of Israel - the Philistines; forbade the Jewish people from entering Jerusalem except on their annual day of mourning, the 9th of the biblical month of Av; and rebuilt Jerusalem as a Roman city, changing its name to Aelia Capitolina.

Who would have thought that the Jewish people would one day inhabit their land again, and that it would be called Israel? Certainly not the nations of the world, who took turns occupying the land and persecuting God's covenant people.

Yet, God never forgot His people or His plan. On the one hand, His prophets spoke of the exile of the people and the deterioration of the land of milk and honey to a land of barrenness at the hands of the enemies of Israel. On the other hand, in His mercy, God also spoke of a prophetic day when His people Israel would be brought back from the four corners of the earth (Isa. 11:11,12), reinhabit their land which would become fruitful again, and find complete spiritual renewal (Ezek. 36). This is that day!

This prophetic process started just over 100 years ago, and is progressing at full force during our lifetime. God is preparing His land and His people for the soon coming of Messiah. The Bible is full of prophetic Scriptures that we are seeing fulfilled before our eyes. The Land of Israel and her people were not just tools of God to be used in days gone by and subsequently discarded. They were, and are, part of God's plan for the redemption of the world along with His Church. His mercies do endure forever. In our day, instead of persecuting the Jewish people, millions of Bible-believing Christians are praying for the peace of Jerusalem and standing in support of God's prophetic plan.

The lessons in this section will put both the Land of Israel and God's Covenant people into biblical context to reveal much to us about God's faithfulness to fulfill His Word and His promises. This should be exciting news for the Church, because if God is faithful to His promises to Israel, then He will be faithful to His promises to the Church. As we both await the coming of Messiah, may we be a part of His plan that will bring blessing to the whole world.

THE LAND IN-BETWEEN
(ISRAEL, GOD'S COVENANTS AND THE CHURCH)

Chapter 9

When I first came to Israel, I traveled around the country walking in the footsteps of the Bible. One day, we were on our way to Tel Megiddo in the Valley of Armageddon. The old bus stopped so that we could see the ancient mound rising from the valley floor. As I got out to get a picture, I noticed the license plate of the bus was 666-666. How appropriate! There I was at the future site of the last great battle between God and the forces of evil. The license plate was a poignant reminder that this was not a fairy tale, but a prophetic event that will one day take place. At that moment I felt like I was in the middle of the bull's eye of a target. Little did I know how true that was.

Megiddo became one of the most important cities of the ancient world because it sat at the crossroads of two great trade routes.

Megiddo is the site of one of the largest and most strategic cities in Solomon's kingdom. In fact, even before it was conquered by Israel, it was an important Canaanite city. This was due to its central location, a factor that will bring it into prominence once again in a prophetic day to come.

Megiddo is located on the southern edge of the great Valley of Esdraelon, also known as the Jezreel Valley and the Valley of Armageddon.

Armageddon is mentioned in Revelation 16:16 as the site of the last great battle between the nations of the world and the Lord Himself. When Napoleon conquered this region in 1799, he assessed this valley as the greatest arena for a battle to be found anywhere in the world. This is because it is ringed by mountains and has entrances at all four compass points.

The name Armageddon comes from the Hebrew words, "Har Megiddon," meaning the Hill of Megiddon. Under this mound are the remains of over 4,000 years of civilization, one layer upon another. Megiddo has witnessed the conquests of every great army to have occupied this region throughout history.

Megiddo was important in the ancient world because it sat at the crossroad of two great trade routes.

Due to the mountains and vast desert to the east of Israel, the main north-south trade route of the ancient world passed right through Israel. It is called the Via Maris (the Way of the Sea) and stretches from Egypt in the southwest to the great kingdoms of the northeast: Assyria, Babylon and Persia. In the days of the Bible, these kingdoms were far more powerful than tiny Israel and when they weren't trading with each other, they were fighting for control of territory. In either case, this route was in constant use.

The east-west trade route allowed travel from the King's Highway in Transjordan westward over the Jordan River through the Beit Shean Valley to the Mediterranean Sea. Megiddo was a place of great influence because it was located where these two routes crossed. In fact, control of this location could control world trade in the ancient world.

Megiddo's significance is a key to why God chose the land of Canaan for the Children of Israel. In fact, one of the best descriptions for Israel could be, *The Land In-Between.*

Israel is actually a hinge — like the hinge on a door — between the great regions of the ancient world: Africa to the south, Asia to the east, Europe and Russia to the north, and the great Mediterranean basin to the west. Whoever controlled the Land of Israel, could exert great influence in the world. That is why conquering Israel was, and still is, a strategic goal of nations seeking to control the Middle East. However, this parcel of land is not up for grabs, because God had, and has, a plan for it.

GOD CHOSE A LAND

In order to determine if today's Israel is located in the same place as biblical Israel, we have to look at the biblical descriptions. What "land" are we talking about? In Genesis 15:18, we are given some dimensions: *"The Lord made a covenant with Abram, saying, 'to your descendants I have given this land, from the river of Egypt, as far as the great river, the river Euphrates.'"*

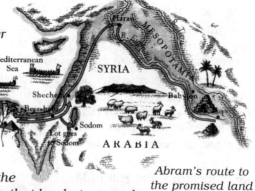

More specifically, Genesis 17:8 states, *"all the Land of Canaan."* In Exodus 3:8, God speaks to Moses in the wilderness and tells him: *"I have come down to deliver them from the power of the Egyptians, and to bring them up to that land...to a good and spacious land...to a land flowing with milk and honey...to the place of the Canaanite and the Hittite,*

Abram's route to the promised land took him along the Fertile Crescent.

and the Amorite and the Perizzite, and the Hivite and the Jebusite."

This description comprises today's Israel, plus part of western Jordan, western Syria, and most of Lebanon.

But, what kind of a land is this Promised Land?

In Exodus 3:8, it is described as, *"...a land flowing with milk and honey."* Then, in Ezekiel 20:6, we read, *"...a land flowing with milk and honey, which is the glory of all lands."*

By the term, "milk and honey," God was describing a land that could sustain animals which produce milk, and flowering, fruitful trees for the bees. And, in the Hebrew Scriptures, honey could also be referring to what we would call fruit jam today, which would further validate the idea of fruit-bearing trees. A land of milk and honey in a desert region would be considered a precious promise from the Lord.

By the term, "glory of all lands," God indicates that Israel would not only be chief among the nations spiritually, but also reflect the other nations of the world temporally in its terrain, flora and fauna.

Let's look at this. Israel is small (150 x 50 miles), but it is blessed with the climate, terrain, and location on earth to sustain vegetation and animal life from four different ecological zones - African, Asian, Mediterranean and Euro-Siberian, as all these zones cross-sect Israel at their extremes.

Israel has lofty mountains, deserts, forests, swamps and seacoasts, and boasts the lowest place on earth. It can support summer, winter and tropical fruits and vegetables. In fact, in Jerusalem you can grow apples and oranges, a cold climate and a tropical fruit all in the same garden! There are twice the plant species in Israel as in its neighbor, Egypt, with the rich Nile Delta. Birds from as far away as South Africa and Iceland spend time in Israel. And, it is visited by the Siberian wolf from the far north and the African leopard from the south.

Truly, Israel is not only the glory of all lands in a spiritual sense, but also physically, as well.

More than this, it is very important to understand that God owns this land. Leviticus 25:23 states: *"The land, moreover, shall not be sold permanently, for the land is Mine, for you are but sojourners with Me."* God holds title to the property. And, in the same way we transfer title of ownership on a car or a house that we own, God chose to transfer title to His land, Israel, to a particular people for all time.

God chose a man, Abraham, to possess His Land, Israel, because He had a plan: the redemption of the world. This was accomplished through the descendants of Abraham, Isaac and Jacob, just as He promised.

GOD CHOSE A PEOPLE

Nearly 4,000 years ago, God called a man named Abram for a special task. Originally from Ur of the Chaldees, (near Basra, Iraq today), he was living in Haran, in today's southern Turkey, when God called him. When he was 75 years old, God spoke to Abram: *"Get out of your country, and from your kindred, and from your father's house, unto a land that I will show you; And I will make of you a great nation, and I will bless you and make your name great; and you will be a blessing. And I will bless them that bless you, and curse him that curses you: and in you will all the families of the earth be blessed"* (Gen. 12:1-3).

Abram, his barren wife Sarai, and nephew Lot left Haran for Canaan where God said to him: *"Lift up your eyes from where you are and look north and south, east and west. All the land that you see I will give to you and your descendants forever. I will make your descendants like the dust of the earth, so that if anyone could count the dust, then your descendants could be counted. Go, walk through the length and breadth of the land, for I am giving it to you"* (Gen. 13:14-17).

Ten years after Abram and Sarai waited in Canaan for the promised offsping, they became impatient. Sarai offered her handmaid,

Ishmael and Isaac were destined to inherit separate kingdoms.

Hagar, to Abram, and they had a son whom they named Ishmael. However, this was not the promised son.

Isaac, the Promised Son: Finally, fourteen years later (24 years after their arrival in Canaan), God spoke to Abram about His promise. It was then God changed Abram's name to Abraham, and Sarai's name to Sarah, as He began to unfold the rest of His promise. In Genesis 17:7-8,

God says, *"I will establish My covenant as an everlasting covenant between Me and you and your descendants after you for the generations to come, to be your God and the God of your descendants after you. The whole land of Canaan, where you are now an alien, I will give as an everlasting possession to you and your descendants after you; and I will be their God."* This confirms that God's covenant was everlasting and unconditional, not temporary. At this point, Abraham was 99 years old, and Sarah was 90 years old and still barren. Because of this, he got the idea that Ishmael, who was his son, would be the carrier of the promise. In Genesis 17:18, Abraham said to God, *"Oh, that Ishmael might live before you."*

This was not God's plan, which He explained: Ishmael was not the promised son and Sarah would, in fact, have a child: Isaac, who would be heir and possessor of the promises and the deed to the land. To Abraham's inquiry, God said, *"No, but Sarah, your wife, shall bear you a son, and you shall call his name Isaac; and I will establish My covenant with him for an everlasting covenant for his descendants after him"* (Gen. 17:19).

What about Ishmael? Isn't he too a son of Abraham? Yes, but not the son of promise.

God went on to say, *"And as for Ishmael, I have heard you: I will surely bless him:... I will make him into a great nation. But My covenant I will establish with Isaac, whom Sarah will bear to you by this time next year"* (Gen. 17:20-21).

Read this verse again. Isaac was to receive the covenant blessing, not Ishmael. This brings us right up to date, because a burning issue today is, "Whose Land is Israel - the Arabs or the Jews?" God promised to greatly bless Ishmael and his descendants, but not with the land of Canaan which God deeded to Abraham's descendants via Isaac. This is a critical point since many Arabs claim a right to the land of Israel as descendants of Abraham through Ishmael's line! As descendants of Abraham via Ishmael, they may receive many promised blessings, but NOT the land of Israel. That is for the descendants of Abraham, Isaac and Jacob.

We also know that Abraham had other sons who also were NOT given rights in the land of Canaan. In Genesis 25:1-6, we read that Abraham's other sons were given gifts and sent away to lands in the east: *"Abraham left everything he owned to Isaac. But while he was still living he gave gifts to the sons of his concubines and sent them away from his son Isaac to the land of the east."*

Jacob, the Promised Son: Later, Isaac had two sons, Jacob and Esau, and we read a similar promise God made to Jacob. In Genesis 35:11-12, God says to Jacob: *"I am God Almighty; Be fruitful and multiply; A nation and a company of nations shall come from you, and kings come forth from you. And the land which I gave to Abraham and Isaac, I will give it to you, And I will give the land to your descendants after you."*

What about Esau? In Genesis 36:6-9, we learn that Esau took his family and moved out of the Land of Canaan away from Jacob. The reason is that he was so rich that the land could not sustain all of his animals. He moved to the Land of Edom, across the Dead Sea (the southern part of today's Kingdom of Jordan).

Covenantally and historically, the land of Israel scripturally belongs to the Jews, the descendants of Abraham, Isaac, and Jacob.

Yet, have the Arabs been cheated? God said He would bless them, and today, there are 21 sovereign Arab states and just ONE Jewish state.

And, the combined land area of the Arab world is 650 times larger than Israel. In other terms, Israel is the same size as the US state of New Jersey, or Wales. However, the Arab states are one and a half million square miles larger than the U.S.A., and they still control much of today's oil supplies. (That's a land area the size of the U.S., including Alaska and Hawaii, and 3/4 of Canada opposed to the state of New Jersey.) No, the Arabs have not been cheated, simply because the Jews have returned to their ancient homeland in Israel.

GOD HAD A PLAN

There was an important reason for God to establish His covenants with His chosen people in His chosen land.

You see, God chose a particular place, Israel, and a particular people, the descendants of Abraham, Isaac, and Jacob, for a particular purpose.

The Jewish people were chosen:

1) To witness to the unity of God in the midst of universal idolatry.

2) To show the nations the blessedness of serving the true God.

3) To receive, preserve, and transmit the Scriptures, (64 of the 66 books of the Bible were written by Jewish writers), and,

4) To be the human channel for the Messiah, the Savior of the world.

This land, chosen by God, was also selected for a special reason. As I already mentioned, it is strategically located right smack in the middle of the crossroads of the ancient world with all of its challenges. And this is right where God wanted His people to be. As they say in the advertising business: location, location, location.

God put His chosen people in a precarious place, right where God wanted them for a chosen purpose. At times of war or at times of peace, God's message would get out to the known world.

But why? God could have taken them to the remotest desert of the Middle East and created another Garden of Eden for them. There, they could have just basked in God's glory and provision, being removed from the conflicts of the world. In fact, out in the driest part of the desert where no one travels, they could have gone unnoticed until this century when our satellites would have finally photographed them from above.

God had other plans.

1. The strategic location of the land would create special pressures. You might call it, "God's testing ground of faith." In this land, there was much pressure and many tests. But, through these tests, with all odds against the Israelites, God showed forth His miracle power to sustain them and bless them, even in difficult situations. That made people sit up and take notice.

2. Since all communication, trade, and even armies of the ancient world had to pass through this land, the message of God's relationship to man through His chosen people would be spread to the known world.

The people of Israel were to be the living testimony of God through their lifestyle and message.

In times of peace, traders and travelers could see and hear God's message to take to the world.

At times of war, God showed His power to miraculously defend them. This message also went around the world. For example, the great King Sennacherib of Assyria invaded Judah in 701 BC. When he reached Jerusalem, he blockaded the city and mocked King Hezekiah and the God of Israel. God moved. The angel of the Lord killed the soldiers and officers of Sennacherib. II Chronicles 32 says that Sennacherib returned back to Assyria in disgrace. Not only is this recorded in the Bible, but Sennacherib left an account of this event chiseled in stone which testifies to what God did on this day in Israel.

WHAT DOES ALL THIS MEAN TO US?

God's eternal, redemptive plan is clear in the Bible. Man sinned, separating himself from God. Yet, God wants to fellowship with us, so He implemented a plan that involved a man, Abraham, and a land, Israel, to bring about the salvation of the world.

However, this plan is not finished and the fulfillment of God's prophetic Word is taking place and relates to Israel and the Jewish people today. No doubt, there was, and is, a destiny that has shaped the history of the world.

We, as Christians, are part of this destiny. In Ephesians 2:12-13, Paul is talking to us Gentiles, saved by grace, about our relationship to Israel and God's covenants and promises made to His people Israel. He says, "remember that at that time you were separate from Christ (Messiah), excluded from citizenship in Israel and foreigners to the covenants of the promise, without hope and without God in the world. But now, in Christ Jesus (Yeshua HaMeshiach), you who once were far away have been brought near through the blood of Christ." In other words, we are fellow citizens of Israel; and its current and future destiny, as God prepares His land and His people for the soon coming of Messiah, should be of utmost importance to us today.

Also, the people of Israel were chosen to be a testimony for God. They did not have books, tapes, radio and television, as we do today. Their lives were a living message to the world.

This is also true for us as Christians. Paul says of us in II Corinthians 3:2,3: "You yourselves are our letter, written on our hearts, known and read by everybody. You show that you are a letter from Messiah, the result of our ministry, written not with ink, but with the Spirit of the living God, not on tablets of stone, but on tablets of human hearts."

Like Israel, when we are born into the Kingdom of God, He does not remove us from the pressures of life. Rather, He puts us into a busy intersection of life, with traffic swirling all around us. There, He blesses us. And, when problems arise, He is there to protect and defend us. In both cases, this becomes a testimony to the living God, whom we serve.

Consider Joshua, who was called to bring the Children of Israel into the Promised Land. Not only was the land promised, but God defined the borders of each tribal area. It is so accurate that you can read the account of this division in the Book of Joshua today and trace the borders, valley for valley, hill for hill, on the modern map of Israel. This was no fairy tale, but God's provision for His Chosen People and His Chosen Land. But was it easy for Joshua? Not at all. Starting with Jericho, they had to fight every step of the way to conquer that which God provided for them. Was God in this? Yes, He was. Through it He showed His power to His people and also to His enemies. *"Nothing is impossible with God"* (Lk. 1:37). The key to this passage is that God has the means to make the impossible, possible. As we abide in Him, we can see His victory in our lives.

Nevertheless, God never promised that He would put us into heaven on earth - that will come in eternity. Here on earth, we are called to walk out our salvation and be a witness of Him. We have an opportunity to do this each day, and should not depend on someone or something else to do the job for us.

Like Israel, we need to be rooted and grounded in the Lord, lest our enemies overrun us, or famine and drought overcome us. This is what happened when Israel took their eyes off the Lord. Only as we abide in the Lord, will we find His provision and protection that will amaze the world around us and bring others into God's kingdom.

Like Israel, we are not an island unto ourselves. We are standing in the crossroads of life, so we can bring glory to His Name.

This Lesson from the Land of the Bible is found in our
Jerusalem Mosaic Video Series, Program #109,
along with other exciting features.
Please turn to page 186 to order your copy.

THE FLOWERS OF ISRAEL SPEAK...

Chapter 10

I just love spring and early summer in Israel. After the winter rains, the hills of Israel, even in the Judean desert, are covered with green grass and an abundance of beautiful wildflowers.

Pat, Ashley, Allison and I (my wife and two daughters) love to go to an archaeological site near our home and walk the terraces on the hills that surround it. The site has yet to be excavated, and we can walk around the foundations of ancient homes and buildings protruding from the soil, imagining what it must have been like to live there thousands of years ago. We come with our wildflower book, and observe an unbelievable variety of gorgeous wildflowers. Some we pick and press to look at later. Others are protected, and we just look at them and record the event in our book.

What we are seeing reminds us of the words of Isaiah, when he said, *"The wilderness and the solitary place will be glad for them and the desert will rejoice and blossom as a rose"* (Isa. 35:1). He wrote these words to express the excitement there would be when the Jewish people would return to their ancient homeland, Israel. Even the land would burst forth with joy.

You may ask, return from where? Many Old Testament prophets spoke of a day when most of the Jewish people would be exiled from Israel. This occurred shortly after the time of Jesus. But God did not intend to leave them in exile, and the prophets foretold of their return from the nations of the world in a future day.

That day is today. We are living in a day when Bible prophecy is being fulfilled right before our eyes. As we prepare for the coming of the Lord, the Bible gives us signs to be watching for. One of these signs is Israel's deserts and vacant places blooming. And blooming, they are.

Although this is a desert climate, after the winter rains and warm spring sunlight, the desert comes to life on its own. Some very delicate flowers such as orchids, cyclamen, wild irises, crocuses, and even wild tulips create a carpet of vivid color along with lush green grass. People are surprised to discover that tulips originally came from this part of the world and were perfected by the Dutch. Everywhere you can find clusters of little red, poppy-like anemones. These are the lilies-of-the-field that we read about in Matthew 6:28 and Luke 12:27.

The abundance and variety of the flowers depends on the quantity of rain. Sometimes the seeds and bulbs remain dormant for years until there is enough rain, and then they bloom. This is particularly true in the far reaches of the desert. It is amazing that these delicate and beautiful visual gifts from the Lord remain tightly packaged in the hard, dry ground until the right conditions prevail. Then they burst forth in an explosion of color and beauty, which lasts for only a few weeks. Some varieties are gone in just a few days.

On the way to the Dead Sea, near the Good Samaritan Inn, we find an amazing sight each spring. There, in the usually bleak desert, the lilies-of-the-field are ablaze in a carpet of red. They bloom in the millions and are a stark contrast to the barren, sandy-brown color of the rest of the year. This all takes place within a couple of weeks, and then it is back to the desert.

Israel has 3,000 varieties of plants, twice as many varieties as in neighboring Egypt, which boasts the fertile Nile Valley. God has really blessed this tiny land with varieties of vegetation, more than any other country in this region of the world.

Not only do Israel's deserts burst forth each spring, but Israel grows flowers in the desert all year around. In the sun-parched landscape, literally tens of millions of flowers of many varieties are grown and exported around the world.

IT HASN'T ALWAYS BEEN THIS WAY

In the 1860s, when Mark Twain traveled in what was then a backward region of the Ottoman Turkish Empire, called Palestine, this is how he described the land: *"Nowhere in all the waste around was there a foot of shade,"* He called the land a *"blistering naked treeless land."* Of the Galilee, he said, *"It is seven in the morning, and as we are in the country, the grass ought to be sparkling with dew, the flowers enriching the air with their fragrance, and the birds singing in the trees. But, alas, there is no dew here, nor flowers, nor birds, nor trees. There is a plain and an unshaded lake, and beyond them some barren mountains."*

Mark Twain

Mark Twain's summary of Palestine: *"Of all the lands there are for dismal scenery, I think Palestine must be the prince. The hills are barren, they are dull of color, they are unpicturesque in shape. It is a hopeless, dreary, heartbroken land."* This description matches that of Ezekiel 36:1-7.

GOD'S PROMISE TO ISRAEL

Despite the fact that most of the Jewish people were dispersed from the Land of Israel by the Romans and are found in almost every nation of the world, that was not God's original plan. God intended for them to be in the land of promise, Israel, where both they and the land would flourish (Gen. 17:8).

Reading Ezekiel 36 is like reading today's newspaper. It gives us a remarkably clear and prophetic picture of what has taken place over the past 120 years. Interestingly, today's wildflowers on the hills of Israel have a lot to do with it, and testify to God's faithfulness.

Ezekiel 36 is one of my favorite chapters

"For I will take you out of the nations; I will gather you from all the countries and bring you back into your own land" (Eze. 36:24).

in the Bible, because it is a faithful promise to Israel concerning God's restoration of the land and the people of Israel in the days just before the coming of the Lord.

This passage opens with God speaking to the mountains of Israel, lamenting at their desolation caused by Israel's enemies who invaded the land to conquer the *"ancient high places"* and then boast about it. He did not intend that His land, Israel, was to be inhabited by any other people, and so it lay barren for generations. The observations of Mark Twain aptly fit the prophet's lament.

But, in v. 8, God had exciting news for the land, *"But you, O mountains of Israel, you will shoot forth your branches and yield your fruit to My people Israel; for they are soon to come home."*

He went on to say that He would multiply the numbers of people from the house of Israel, they would rebuild the ruined and wasted cities, and increase their flocks and produce of the land. When this happens, He says, *"You will know that I am the Lord."*

There is a connection between the fruitfulness of the land of Israel and those inhabiting it. God owns the land (Lev. 25:23) and chose to give it to His covenant people - the Jewish people, the descendants of Abraham,

Isaac and Jacob. Only when the land and the covenant people are together in combination, do both flourish in accordance with God's divine plan.

Ezekiel confirms that it is the return of the Jewish people to the Land of Israel that triggers the restoration of the land itself to its former glory - and more.

Their return and the land's restoration was also important for God's integrity, as well.

In judgment, God scattered His covenant people for a season. Once scattered, Ezekiel 36:20 tells us that the scattered people of Israel profaned the integrity of the Lord's Name and His promises among the nations, when the nations said, *"These are the people of the Lord, and they had to leave His land."*

You see, in the ancient world, the pagans judged the effectiveness of their pagan gods by how well the gods protected them in their land and provided for them. Various gods were sought for:

1) SECURITY of their land from invading armies (e.g., Ba'al, the god of war and thunder);

2) RAIN and FOOD versus drought and famine (e.g., Ba'al); and,

3) OFFSPRING to care for them in their old age (e.g., Astarte, the goddess of fertility).

(Mankind still has the tendency to evaluate how well "god" is taking care of them by prosperity at home and the lack of trouble.)

Therefore, when the Jewish people went into exile and the land became desolate, the pagan nations mocked the God of Israel as unable to provide for His people.

For this reason, in Ezekiel 36:23-28, God speaks of a great end-time return of the Jewish people to their covenant land, which He will orchestrate for the integrity of His Name, to show the nations of the world that He is the God who keeps His promises.

To accomplish this, in verse 24, God says, *"For I will take you out of the nations; I will gather you from all the countries and bring you back into your own land."*

In addition, God also desires to restore spiritual fellowship with His people IN His land when He says in verses 27-28, *"And I will put My Spirit in you and move you to follow My decrees and be careful to keep My laws. You will live in the land I gave your forefathers; and you will be My people and I will be your God."*

The process of this latter-day, prophetic move, as expressed by Ezekiel, is what I call the three R's of end-time Bible prophecy concerning Israel:

- a RETURN from exile to the land of their forefathers;
- the RESTORATION of the land, and then,
- the REDEMPTION and renewal of their spiritual life as a people in the land.

Yes, this day is today! The rabbis themselves refer to our present day as "Messianic Days." Surely, the land IS being restored and the people have been returning for over 100 years. And, as the Jewish immigrants return, many from former communist lands where the worship of God and the reading of the Bible was forbidden, they are now learning of the Lord God of Israel back in their ancient homeland, and a true spiritual renewal is taking place. It is not all happening at once, but it is certainly in process.

Despite the problems in Israel, God is doing a work in the hearts of His people, which is also reflected in the land. Just as in days of old, as the people of Israel walk in God's light, He is the One who sustains His land and His people. *"If you walk in My statutes, and keep My commandments, and do them; Then I will give you rain in due season, and the land shall yield her increase, and the trees of the field shall yield their fruit"* (Lev. 26:1,2).

Ezekiel gives us God's last word to the heathen nations of the world who sought to occupy His land and prevent His people from returning: *"The desolate land will be cultivated instead of lying desolate in the sight of all who pass through it. They will say, 'This land that was laid waste has become like the garden of Eden; the cities that were lying in ruins, desolate and destroyed, are now fortified and inhabited. Then the nations around you that remain will know that I, the Lord, have rebuilt what was destroyed and have replanted what was desolate. I the Lord have spoken, and I will do it'"* (Eze. 36:34-36).

THE MESSAGE OF THE WILDFLOWERS

You know, nothing much happens in Israel that is not related to the Scriptures. God often uses the obvious and observable to teach us, so that His lessons are reinforced over and over - each time we see and are reminded.

We are celebrating a prophetic restoration that is coming to pass, as a testimony to God's faithfulness. No longer is the land desolate and devoid of His covenant people. Today, we see the hills of Israel covered with beautiful wildflowers and lush green grass, abundant fields of produce, new cities rebuilt on ancient sites, cattle on the hills, birds in the trees, and the Jewish people who have returned from over 100 nations and are still returning at the rate of 4,000 to 6,000 a month.

Yes, the day Ezekiel talked about is today! As I walk the hills with my family simply looking at the wildflowers covering the land, I see in them an incredible message. We are walking in a modern-day miracle wrought by the hand of God. Isaiah 35:1 says of this return, *"The wilder-*

ness and the wasteland will be glad for them, and the desert will rejoice and blossom as a rose!" While Israel has not yet seen the complete fulfillment of these prophecies, their fulfillment certainly needs to be the focus of our prayers for Israel.

For those of us who honor the Bible, let us stand with Israel with our prayers and our voices as God fulfills His prophetic Word. There are those who constantly challenge Israel's right to exist. But, God says they won't prevail. Psalm 129:5-6 says, *"May all who hate Zion be turned back in shame. May they be like grass on the housetops, which withers before it can grow..."*

From my house, we look down upon a small Arab village in the valley below. On the roofs of several old stone houses, we can see grass growing in abundance during the winter rains. But, as its roots dry up from lack of water, this grass quickly turns brown. So too, those who mock or disregard God's Word will also quickly wither and fade away, but God's Word will prevail.

History is becoming increasingly focused on Israel and especially on Jerusalem. As Christians, we have an incredible opportunity to reach out and touch Israel and the Jewish people in tangible ways to show them "the love of God" and "the God of love."

As you enjoy the beautiful flowers where you live, may God remind you often of the "Message of the Wildflowers." May He remind you to *"pray for the peace of Jerusalem"* (Ps. 122:6). Our God is faithful and true, and He is completing His work here in Israel, just as He promised and right on schedule!

This Lesson from the Land of the Bible is found in our
Jerusalem Mosaic Video Series, Program #105,
along with other exciting features.
Please turn to page 186 to order your copy.

THE THRESHING FLOOR

Chapter 11

Probably the most hotly contested spot on earth is the ancient Temple Mount of Jerusalem. While today two Moslem mosques rest there, it is the site of Solomon's and Herod's Temples where the presence of God Himself dwelled in the Holy of Holies. The fact that Moslem mosques are there at all, one of them being a former Byzantine church, is because of the connection of this site with the presence of the God of the Bible. The Palestinians are in total control of this area today, yet there are many religious Jews who see this site as central to Jewish worship, and hope and pray that one day it will again be in Jewish hands. Because the ancient Temple area is so holy to them, a small remnant of the external retaining wall of Herod's Temple platform, known today as the Western Wall, is considered a sacred area.

Is there any significance to this location being chosen for God's temple? Of course, God always has a purpose for what He does.

KING DAVID, JERUSALEM, AND THE TEMPLE MOUNT

It was God's plan that King David would unite the tribes of Israel. In order to do this, God chose the city of Jerusalem, which was on the border of the tribes of Benjamin and Judah. It was centrally located and provided an administrative center from which to run the kingdom. In II Samuel 5, we see that David left his capital in Hebron and was led by the Lord to conquer Jerusalem from the Jebusites.

"Then King David and his men marched to Jerusalem to attack the Jebusites, who lived there.... David then took up residence in the fortress

and called it the City of David. He built up the area around it, from the sup-
porting terraces inward. And he became more and more powerful, because
the Lord God Almighty was with him" (II Sam. 5:6a, 9-10).

More important than being just an administrative center, God
desired Jerusalem to be a spiritual center where His presence would dwell
in a Temple built for Him. Because David was a man of war with blood on
his hands, God gave the task of building the Temple to David's son,
Solomon, even giving him specifications for the design. However, even
though Solomon built the Temple, David prepared the place.

In II Chronicles 3:1, we read, *"Then Solomon began to build the Tem-*
ple of the Lord in Jerusalem on Mount Moriah, where the Lord had
appeared to his father David. It was on the threshing floor of Araunah the
Jebusite, the place provided by David."

We read in II Samuel 24 and I Chronicles 21 that David bought this
threshing floor. David had sinned before the Lord, and the prophet Gad
brought a word from the Lord that David should build an altar to the
Lord, on the threshing floor of Araunah. There, he was to offer burnt
offerings and peace offerings to stop a plague that had afflicted the people of Israel because of David's sin.

Araunah gladly offered the location, his oxen for the offering, and
his threshing sled and implements as wood for the fire.

In II Samuel 24:24 we read, *"But the king replied to Araunah, 'No, I*
insist on paying you for it. I will not sacrifice to the Lord my God burnt offer-
ings that cost me nothing.'"

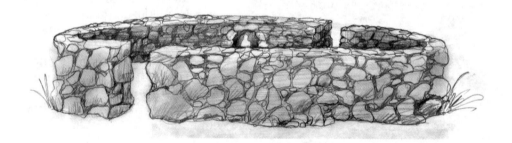

THE SIGNIFICANCE OF
THE THRESHING FLOOR

This location, which became the site of God's Temple, was and is
significant.

- First, it was chosen by God.
- Second, it was a prominent high place in Jerusalem that over-
  looked the City of David, making it easy to be seen by all.
- Thirdly, it was a threshing floor which is rich in meaning. Let's
  look at this.

A threshing floor was generally on a high place surrounded by a low stone wall, often where bedrock was exposed on a high hill. Here, it was easy to catch the wind necessary to blow the chaff away from the kernels of wheat that were tossed high in the air during the winnowing process. The bedrock could be easily swept to provide a clean place to catch the falling kernels for collection and storage.

Because food was not available to the ancients, as we have today in our 24-hour-a-day supermarkets with unending supplies of local and imported foods, every kernel of wheat was important. People never knew when there might be a famine, so they always thanked their gods for the provision of food, in hopes that they would provide for another year.

Therefore, in the ancient world, the threshing floor became a logical site for pagans to build small niches in which to place stone and wood idols of Baal or Astarte, the goddess of fertility. These little idols got the credit for God's provision of food.

THE THRESHING FLOOR AND HIGH PLACES

In the Bible, we often read about the high places being places of worship to pagan gods. God wanted these destroyed in Israel as they were an abomination. Many of these high places were threshing floors where pagans worshipped their gods. But, it was not only the pagans. Sadly, like us, even the Israelites were not immune to worshipping an idol, just for insurance, and thereby angering God.

Archaeologists have excavated Israelite houses in the hills of Samaria and found idols such as those hidden under the floor stones of the house. The Israelites, seeing the prosperity of the world in the lives of pagans living around them, were tempted to live according to the ways of the world.

Therefore, when God placed His house, His Temple, on the threshing floor of Araunah, He was making a very loud statement to the ancients.

1) He is Yahweh Yireh, often mispronounced as Jehovah Jireh, God who is the provider. He is the giver of the Bread of Life, and the sustainer of life.

2) There are no other gods before the Lord God of Israel. It is He who is the King of kings and Lord of lords, and who alone is to be worshiped on the high place of Jerusalem.

Thus, there was something very significant about David buying the threshing floor of Araunah. It became a focal point for Israel and the world, as it

Baal Peor, Canaanite deity worshipped by Israelites during their wanderings in the desert.
(Num. 25)

was the place of worship to the Lord God of Israel. Here, pagan gods were supplanted by the Most High God. David had to buy it since God's temple could not rest on pagan-owned land.

THE TEMPLE MOUNT CHOSEN BY GOD

Yes, this site was chosen by God, and bought with silver and gold by King David 3,000 years ago, when Jerusalem was established as the eternal capital of Israel.

It was at this site that God's presence dwelled in Jerusalem for over a thousand years. And it is to this place that the Lord will return to establish His kingdom in Israel. From here, He will rule and reign in the earth, from Jerusalem.

Today, we find on this same Temple Mount a Moslem mosque with the area completely controlled by Moslem authorities. Jews and Christians are not allowed to pray at this site and are removed by Moslem authorities, if they attempt to pray there.

Nevertheless, no matter what the Moslems say, no matter what the United Nations, the Palestinian Authority or anybody else says, the Jewish people still own this Temple Mount. David bought it, it has been recorded for all time, and the deed is still valid.

In the fulfillment of Bible prophecy, the Jewish people have come back into this land by the millions. Does it seem likely that they should continue to be relegated to worshiping God only at a small section of an outer retaining wall of the Temple Mount - known as the Western Wall?

Many Christians believe that day is coming when the God of the Bible will be honored on top of the Mount again. From here, the Lord will be worshipped in a Third Temple that is yet to be built on the site, and Messiah will rule and reign from Jerusalem. When and how this will occur, only God knows.

Meanwhile this place, that once was a lowly threshing floor, remains a place of utmost importance even to this prophetic day, as all of history is becoming increasingly focused on Israel and Jerusalem.

This Lesson from the Land of the Bible is found in our
Jerusalem Mosaic Video Series, Program #110,
along with other exciting features.
Please turn to page 186 to order your copy.

THE RETURN TO ZION
ISAIAH 11:11-12

Chapter 12

Was the covenant God made with the descendants of Abraham, Isaac and Jacob to last forever?

Did God promise that the Jews, dispersed into the world, would one day return to their ancestral land?

Did God describe the condition of the land before their return, and then tell what would happen to it once the Jewish people came home?

Is the modern State of Israel connected to biblical Israel?

If so, as God arranged for Joshua to bring the Children of Israel into the Promised Land, how has God arranged for the Jewish people to come back home in our day?

A number of Christians have asked me these questions about the establishment of the modern State of Israel. To get the answer, we need to look more closely at the modern history of Israel so we can see how God has remained faithful to His covenant promises with Israel, fulfilling His prophetic Word.

Many Christians visiting Israel have expressed to me, "It sure would have been exciting to have visited Israel in 'the Bible days,' when God was really doing something here."

I always reply, "These *are* 'Bible days,' and God is definitely at work today!" In fact, it has been suggested that there are more Bible prophecies affecting global events being fulfilled in our generation, than at any other time in history.

Surely, this is an exciting Bible topic for us to explore together.

This Hagana ship is typical of the many overcrowded ships that ran the British blockade to bring thousands of immigrants home to Israel.

117

ISRAEL AND THE BIBLE

First, let us look at the scriptural record concerning God's covenantal connection to Israel and the Jewish people: past, present and future.

After man had fallen into sin, God implemented His plan for the salvation of the world. He found a man (Abraham), and told him the He would take him to a land that He would show him (Israel). Through Abraham and his descendants, God had a plan to bless the whole world.

In Genesis 12:1-3, we see God outlining His plan to bless the whole world through Abraham and his descendants. *"The Lord said to Abram, 'Leave your country, your people and your father's household and go to the land I will show you. I will make you into a great nation and I will bless you; I will make your name great and you will be a blessing. I will bless those that bless you and whoever curses you, I will curse; and all peoples on earth will be blessed through you.'"*

God confirmed this covenant with Abraham, and his son Isaac, and his grandson, Jacob. It was through this specific bloodline that the covenant with the land and a people would pass. *"And I will establish My covenant between Me and you and your descendants after you throughout their generations for an everlasting covenant, to be God to you and to your descendants after you. And I will give to you and to your descendants after you, the land of your sojournings, all the land of Canaan, for an everlasting possession; and I will be their God"* (Gen. 17:7-8).

It was through the Jewish people, God's Chosen or Covenant people, that we received our salvation.

They were chosen to live in God's land, Israel, to worship God and be blessed by Him, thus showing the world the blessedness of serving the one true God.

They were also chosen to hear, receive and record God's Word so we could have the Bible - 64 of the 66 books of the Bible were written by Jewish writers.

And, it was through them that Messiah would come to save Israel and the world.

This covenant with the land and a people, the Jewish people, was an everlasting covenant. While their quality of life on that land was conditional, the attachment to that land was unconditional. *"This is what the Lord says, He who appoints the sun to shine by day, who decrees the moon and stars to shine by night, who stirs up the sea so that its waves roar - the Lord Almighty is His Name, 'Only if these decrees vanish from My sight,' declares the Lord, 'will the descendants of Israel ever cease to be a nation before Me'"* (Jer. 31:35-36). Each time Israel sinned, they were either judged or exiled, but God, in His mercy, has always brought them back to full status in the land. The sun, moon and stars are still shining in the heavens, and so today, Israel is still a nation and God has shown His faithfulness to His Word.

While we know about the exiles and returns of the Jewish people recorded in the Bible, what do we know about the last 2,000 years of Israel's history?

After the time of Jesus, there were two Jewish revolts against Rome, which resulted in the destruction of Herod's Temple and much of Jerusalem, it ultimately being rebuilt as a Roman city. And, because the Romans wanted to erase the God-given connection between the land and the Jewish people, the Emperor Hadrian renamed the land Palestine, after the arch-enemies of David, the Philistines.

From the last great exile under the Romans until the late 1800s, even though there was a small Jewish presence in the land, the bulk of the Jewish people lived outside the land in what is called the Diaspora.

Nevertheless, God said that just before Messiah would come, He would bring His people back to Israel and restore that land in preparation for this great event. Not only has God preserved His people, Israel, but also His covenant land. Ancient Israel and modern Israel are both part of God's great redemptive plan.

There are a multitude of Bible prophecies concerning the regathering of the Jewish people from exile around the world to a barren land that would be restored to its former glory:

Isaiah 11:11,12 says: *"In that day, the Lord will reach out His hand a second time to reclaim the remnant that is left of His people... He will raise a banner from the nations and gather the exiles of Israel; He will assemble the scattered people of Judah from the four quarters of the earth."*

Isaiah 35:1 says: *"The wilderness and the solitary place will be glad for them and the desert will blossom as a rose."*

Amos 9:14,15 says: *"I will bring back My exiled people Israel; they will rebuild the ruined cities and live in them. They will plant vineyards and drink their wine; they will make gardens and eat their fruit. I will plant Israel in their own land, never again to be uprooted from the land I have given them.' says the Lord your God."*

Ezekiel 36 gives us the most complete description of the condition of the land and the people just before its restoration. (See chapter 11, "The Flowers of Israel Speak," for a more complete explanation of this exciting prophetic chapter.)

Here, God speaks to a barren, dry land and says that it will be fruitful again, tilled and sown, that His people Israel will return and rebuild their ruined cities and inhabit the waste places (vv. 8-11). God then says He will bring His people, Israel, back home and when the nations round about see this, they will know that He, the Lord God of Israel, has done it for the integrity of His holy Name. God made a covenant promise and He intends to keep it.

There has been a Jewish presence in the Land of Israel for over 3,000 years, ebbing and flowing through its turbulent history, yet always there in some form. While we know much about the period from Abraham through the early first century Church, we are often very unfamiliar with the modern period. Suffice it to say, the Jewish people have remained faithful to their ancestral homeland. Even when exiled from that land, the prayer at every Passover meal was, and is, "Next year in Jerusalem!" The focus of prayers and the cycle of Jewish holidays is always in sync with Israel. For example, Jews living in the southern hemisphere celebrate

Passover (a Spring festival) in March-April, just as it is celebrated in Israel. However, March-April, below the equator, is their fall, not spring.

The multitude of biblical prophecies concerning the regathering of the Jewish people from around the world to a barren land that would be restored to its former glory began to unfold in the late 1800s. Events leading to the establishment of the modern State of Israel began during the period when the Ottoman (Turkish) Empire controlled the region then called Palestine.

TURKISH RULE 1516 - 1917

Under 400 years of harsh Turkish rule, the land was sparsely populated, mostly by nomadic peoples, poorly cultivated and a widely-neglected expanse of eroded hills, sandy deserts, and malarial marshes. Its ancient irrigation systems, terraces, towns and villages had crumbled, and its forests were taxed and cut down to fuel the steam engines carrying goods between Istanbul, Beirut, Damascus and Cairo. "Palestine" was truly a poor, neglected, no-man's land with no important cities, which was administered by absentee landlords.

Mark Twain, who visited Palestine in 1867, described it as a *"...desolate country whose soil is rich enough, but is given over wholly to weeds - a silent mournful expanse ... We never saw a human being on the whole route ... There was hardly a tree or a shrub anywhere. Even the olive and the cactus, those fast friends of a worthless soil, had almost deserted the country." (The Innocents Abroad).*

Mark Twain

The report of the Palestine Royal Commission quotes an account of the Coastal Plain in 1913:

"The road leading from Gaza to the north was only a summer track suitable for transport by camels and carts ... no orange groves, orchards or vineyards were to be seen until one reached Yavne village ... houses were all of mud. Schools did not exist ... The western part, towards the sea was almost a desert ... The villages in this area were few and thinly populated ... many villages were deserted by their inhabitants."

The French author, Voltaire, described Palestine as, *"a hopeless, dreary place."* In short, under the Turks, the land suffered both from neglect and a low population.

Today, the land is rejoicing with life which has come back to the country since the Jewish people began their return in the late 1800s. Isaiah 35:1 states, *"The wilderness and the solitary place shall be glad for them, and the desert will blossom as a rose."* Each spring, even the barren desert blooms into bright color as green grass and multi-colored flowers carpet the landscape in apparent celebration, just as is prophesied in the Bible.

This process has not been without its difficulties. However, when we read the book of Joshua, we see that even though God said He was bringing the Israelites into their Promised Land, the movement into the land was not without its great problems. The enemies of the Bible and God's plans are always in opposition to it.

In the 1880s, during the Turkish period, Jews began to immigrate to Palestine from Yemen in the south and Russia in the north, Morocco in the west, and Iraq in the east. This move into Israel was the beginning of the fulfillment of the prophetic return to Zion, which has been taking place over the past 120 years in a series of *Aliyot*, or large moves of Jewish populations into the land of Israel. (*Aliyah* is a Hebrew term for "going up" or immigration.)

Forty-five thousand Yemenite Jews, almost every Jewish person in Yemen, were flown to Israel during "Operation Magic Carpet" in the early 1950s.

Nevertheless, the many, many difficulties have not prevented the Jewish people from coming home to Zion, by the millions.

The First Aliyah started in the 1880s when new communities began to spring up, including Petah Tikva, Rosh Pinna, Rishon le Zion, Gedera, and Zichron Ya'acov. Jews purchased land at high prices, 73% of it from the absentee Arab landlords who lived in Cairo, Damascus and Beirut. About 80% of the Arabs living in Palestine came in to work for these landlords and were debt-ridden peasants, semi-nomads and Bedouins. (A. Granott, *The Land System in Palestine*, London, 1952.) Most of the land purchased had not been cultivated previously because it was swampy, rocky, sandy, or for some other reason, regarded as uncultivable.

According to the Peel Commission (1937): *"The Arab charge that the Jews have obtained too large a proportion of good land cannot be maintained. Much of the land now carrying orange groves was sand dunes or swamp and uncultivated when it was purchased."*

Moreover, the price the Jews paid for this barren land was exorbitant. Moshe Aumann, in his book *Land Ownership in Palestine: 1880-1948*, states: *"In 1944, Jews paid between $1,000 and $1,100 per acre in Palestine, mostly for arid or semi-arid land: in the same year, rich black soil in Iowa was selling for about $110 per acre* (U.S. Dept. of Agriculture)."

In 1897, Jewish leaders, moved by Theodore Herzl, formally organized the Zionist movement at the First Zionist Congress in Basle, Switzerland. They called for the restoration of the Jewish National Home in Palestine where Jews could have sanctuary, self-determination and the renascence of their ancient civilization and culture.

The Second Aliyah, or the second wave of Jewish immigration, took place in the early 1900s. They came from Russia as a result of the Pogroms against the Jewish citizens there. The movie, *Fiddler on the Roof*, depicts Jewish life in Russia at this time, when many were forced to leave — some came to Palestine.

As the Jews immigrated and began to develop the region, Arabs from many parts of the impoverished, decaying Ottoman Empire of the Middle East rushed into Palestine to get jobs. Many of today's "Palestinians" are descendants of these newcomers.

BRITISH RULE: 1917 - 1948

At the beginning of British rule in the Middle East after WWI, there was an effort to reinforce the national aspirations of both the Arabs and Jews of the region. As the Turkish Empire was being dissolved and redivided among various ethnic groups, the horizon looked bright for the creation of a Jewish state in the Middle East.

In 1917, Britain issued the Balfour Declaration:

"His Majesty's Government view with favour the establishment in Palestine of a national home for the Jewish people, and will use their best endeavours to facilitate the achievement of this object, it being clearly understood that nothing shall be done which may prejudice the civil and religious rights of existing non-Jewish communities in Palestine or the rights and political status enjoyed by Jews in any other country."

The Balfour Declaration won the approval of the United States and other Western powers. At first, there was hope that Arabs would also accept it, as both the Arabs and the Jews were just breaking free from the yoke of the Ottoman Empire.

Emir Faisal, son of the acknowledged leader of the Arabs, Sherif Hussein, met with Dr. Chaim Weizmann and other Zionist leaders during the 1919 Paris Peace Conference. They signed an agreement which, *"mindful of the racial kinship and*

Map 1: In 1919, Palestine was considered that portion of the Middle East designated for the Jewish people, and included what we know of today as Jordan, east of the river; and Israel, west of the river.

racial bonds existing between the Arabs and the Jewish people," declared that *"the surest means of working out the consummation of their national aspiration is through the closest possible collaboration of the development of the Arab state and Palestine."* (In 1919, Palestine was considered that portion of the Middle East designated for the Jewish people.) (See Map 1)

The agreement looked to the fulfillment of the Balfour Declaration and also called for *"all necessary measures ... to encourage and stimulate immigration of Jews into Palestine on a large scale, and as quickly as possible to settle Jewish immigrants upon the land through closer settlement and extensive cultivation of the soil."*

On March 3rd, one day after Weizmann presented the Zionist case to the Peace Conference, Faisal wrote to Felix Frankfurter, a U.S. Supreme Court Justice and Zionist leader, declaring:

"The Arabs, especially the educated among us, look with deepest sympathy on the Zionist movement ... We will wish the Jews a hearty welcome home ... We are working together for a reformed and revised Near East and our two movements complete one another. The Jewish movement is nationalist and not imperialist. Our movement is nationalist and not imperialist. And there is room in Syria for us both. (Under Turkish rule, Syria included part of Palestine.) Indeed, I think that neither can be a real success without the other."

Faisal had conditioned his acceptance on the fulfillment of British wartime promises to the Arabs, who had hoped for independence in a vast part of the Ottoman empire.

But these hopes were temporarily dashed when the French took over the mandate for Syria, ejecting Faisal from Damascus, where he had been proclaimed King of Syria. As consolation, the British named

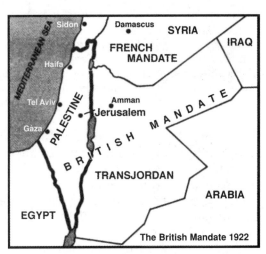

Map 2: In 1922, Palestine was redivided as Transjordan, and Palestine, giving 80% of the Mandate to the Arabs.

Faisal King of Iraq. And in a further effort to please the Arabs, British Colonial Secretary Winston Churchill cut away 80% of the Jewish National Home in Palestine, some 35,000 sq. miles, and created a brand new Arab entity, called Transjordan, and installed Faisal's brother, Abdullah, as Emir. (Abdullah is the grandfather of the present-day King Hussein of Jordan.) Britain administered Transjordan until 1946, when independence was granted, and the name of the area became the Hashemite Kingdom of Jordan. (See Map 2)

This apportionment - the first partition of Palestine and of the promised Jewish National Home - was a blow to the Zionists. The Jewish people reluctantly accepted the partition because Britain simultaneously took over the League of Nations Mandate for Palestine in 1922 and they really had no one to appeal to.

It should be emphasized that Arab hopes for a vast empire have since been realized. Today, the Arab League includes 21 separate Arab states spanning an area of more than 5,000,000 square miles. However, there is only one Jewish state consisting of 8,000 square miles - Israel. (See Map 3)

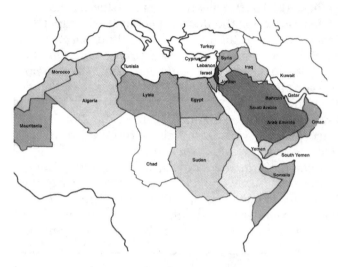

Map 3: Arab hopes for a vast empire have been realized. Today, the Arab League includes 21 separate Arab states spanning an area of more than 5,000,000 square miles. However, there is only one Jewish state consisting of 8,000 square miles - Israel.

While the Arabs showed early signs of acceptance of a Jewish state in Palestine in 1919, later it would be seen that once the Arabs had a taste of independent power, they quickly lost interest in encouraging Jewish immigration and a Jewish state.

Nevertheless, the Third Aliyah began in 1919, motivated by the Balfour Declaration and an open window of opportunity to bring oppressed Jews from eastern Europe and those fleeing communism which was taking control of Russia and surrounding nations. However, during the 1920s, the Arabs had a change of heart and attacks on the Jews of Palestine began in earnest. The fight was on from the Arab side to negate any hope of a Jewish state.

As time went on, the British feared their relations with the Arabs would suffer and sought to protect British oil interests in the Middle East. As World War II loomed on the horizon and oil became a paramount concern, British appeasement to the Arab cause against the Jews of Palestine was obvious. They greatly limited Jewish immigration in the British Mandate.

From 1936-1939, there was an Arab uprising in which 10,000 people were killed. The British showed leniency in the beginning which resulted in a disaster - 1,000 British were killed, 500 Jews, and 8,500 Arabs (most of the Arabs were killed by other Arabs vying for control). In the end, the British had to use the iron-fist policy to stop the uprising. This event put greater fear into the British, who put further limits on Jewish immigration. The climax was the British White Paper in 1939, which ordered that future Jewish immigration be limited to 10,000 per year for five years and to an additional 25,000 refugees from Nazism - 75,000 in all. Hardly much help while Hitler was killing 6,000,000 Jews during this same period. At the end of a ten year period, the White Paper called for an independent state in the region - an Arab state!

During WWII, Haj Amin al-Husseini, the Moslem Mufti of Jerusalem (uncle of today's Palestinian Authority Minister of Jerusalem Affairs, Faisal Husseini), met with Adolph Hitler to organize the extermination of the Jewish populations of the Middle East. Yasser Arafat is also related to this family by his mother.

THE UNITED NATIONS PARTITION PLAN OF 1947

As World War II came to an end, revealing the extent of the catastrophe that had befallen the Jewish people in Europe, there were demands everywhere for swift action to rehabilitate and resettle those who had survived the Holocaust through the establishment of a Jewish state.

The British tried, but failed, to work out an agreement acceptable to both Arabs and Jews, so they turned the problem over to the UN early in 1947.

The UN sent an 11-nation special commission (UNSCOP) to Palestine to investigate. UNSCOP found two people groups, Arabs and Jews, both claiming all the country. To satisfy the national aspirations of both peoples, UNSCOP proposed termination of the British Mandate and a partition of the area into an Arab state and a Jewish state based on population concentrations. Jerusalem would be an international zone. (See map 4) The Jewish state was already in existence in all but name.

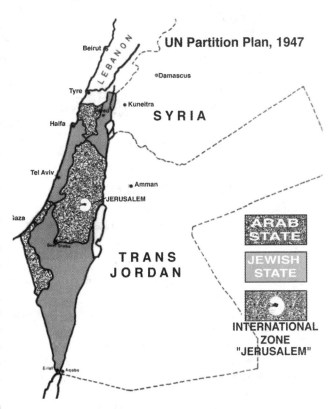

Map 4: The UN proposed a partition of the area into an Arab state and a Jewish state with Jerusalem an international zone. So, eager for independence, the Jews of Palestine were ready to accept a compromise - partition. But the Arabs boycotted the UN plan.

Map 5: In the Arab invasion of 1948 the Arab nations surrounding Israel sought to end all Jewish immigration and destroy the newly declared Jewish State of Israel.

So, eager for independence, the Jews of Palestine were ready to accept a compromise - partition. But the Arabs boycotted the UNSCOP plan.

World opinion strongly favored the UN resolution, and it was adopted by a vote of 33-13, with 10 abstentions, on Nov. 29, 1947.

THE WAR OF 1948

Throughout the 1947 UN debate, the Palestine Arab Higher Commission threatened war, while Jewish Agency spokesmen appealed for peace.

Jamal Husseini, spokesman for the Arab committee, told the UN on Nov. 24, 1947: *"The partition line proposed shall be nothing but a line of fire and blood."*

Five days later, the UN voted for the partition and the Arabs began their war to prevent implementation of the UN resolution. Roads were mined, Jewish settlements isolated, and Jewish convoys were ambushed. By the end of that week, 105 Jews had been killed.

Later, apartments in Jerusalem were blown up and more than 50 men, women and children were killed. Thirty-five Hebrew University students were massacred on the road near Jerusalem. The Jewish Agency was bombed and took heavy casualties. A convoy was set afire on the road to Hadassah Hospital on Mt. Scopus and 77 Jewish doctors, nurses and scientists died.

Nevertheless, on May 14, 1948, the State of Israel was declared to be independent. The Arabs continued to reject the partition and accept their portion of land. Instead, five Arab armies (Egypt, Syria, Transjordan, Lebanon and Iraq) immediately invaded Israel expecting to sweep the Israelis into the sea. On May 15, 1948, Azzam Pasha, Secretary General of the Arab League, said in Cairo: *"This will be a war of extermination and a momentous* massacre which will be spoken of like the Mongolian massacres and the Crusades." (See Maps 5 & 6)

Fortunately, his words were not prophetic and Israel not only retained that which was given to her by the UN, but a bit more. Those areas designated for the Arab state in Palestine were occupied by other Arab countries: the West Bank (of the Jordan River) by Jordan, and the Gaza Strip by Egypt.

After the establishment of the State of Israel, Jewish refugees of WWII and others from Moslem countries of the Middle East began to pour in. From 1948-1972, over 1,400,000 immigrants came into Israel. All had to be settled, trained, given Hebrew language classes, and many needed health care. All of this cost fell on the shoulders of the Israelis and the Jewish community worldwide.

Map 6: In the Armistice Agreement in 1949, the Arabs demanded after defeat, what they could have had before the invasion without firing a shot! The purpose of this declaration by the Arabs was to appear as the defenders of the UN and its resolutions, and to cast Israel as its violator. The opposite was true.

For the Palestinian Arabs of Western Palestine, their rejection of the 1947 partition plan and choosing war caused them to miss the first of many opportunities to obtain a national home — missed by their insistence on a policy of "all or nothing."

In the negotiations for an Armistice Agreement in 1949, the Arabs, having lost, insisted that Israel then accept the 1947 partition lines as borders before they would negotiate. Actually, what they were demanding after defeat, was what they could have had before their invasion without firing a shot! The purpose of this declaration by the Arabs was to appear as the defenders of the UN and its resolutions, and to cast Israel as its violator. The opposite was true.

This model created a novel concept which the Arabs still use to this day: the doctrine of the limited liability war. Under this theory, an aggressor may reject a compromise settlement and may gamble on war to win everything in the comfortable knowledge that, even if he fails, he may insist on reinstating the original compromise and claim rights under it. This has been the pattern in each war of 1948, 1956, 1967, 1973, 1982 and even in today's declarations by Yasser Arafat, head of the Palestinian Authority.

ISRAEL OR PALESTINE?

Currently, Palestine is being defined as only the region west of the Jordan River, that land comprised of Israel, the West Bank and Gaza. The Arab propaganda states that Israel has usurped "all of Palestine," leaving the Palestinian people with nothing. This is simply not the case.

Transjordan's independence, becoming Jordan in 1946, did force an artificial redefinition of "Palestine" to include only that area west of the Jordan River, thus restricting it to 20% of the original Palestine. What the 1947 UN partition did was to further partition the remaining 20% portion into yet another Arab state and a Jewish state. This, however, did not change the fact that Jordan is still part of Palestine, too, with over 70% of its population being Palestinian Arab. (King Hussein is Saudi Arabian, his family having been given this territory by the British after WWI.) With Jordan ignoring the UN partition and annexing the West Bank in 1949, Palestinian Arabs under the Jordanian umbrella controlled 82.5% of the Palestine Mandate given to the Jews, while the Jewish state held a bare 17.5%. (See Map 4)

The Cease Fire Lines After The 1967 Six-Day War

Map 7: In the 1967 Six Day War, Israel was attacked by Egypt and Jordan and won, defensively, the West Bank and Gaza. Jordan lost that war. Nevertheless, Jordan is still a Palestinian Arab state in territory and by population, on 80% of the original Palestine. Despite what the Palestinians say, Israel did not usurp all of Palestine, nor are the Arabs left without a Palestinian state.

In the 1967 Six Day War, Israel was attacked by Egypt and Jordan and won, defensively, the West Bank and Gaza. (See map 7) Jordan lost that war. Nevertheless, Jordan is still a Palestinian Arab state in territory and by population, on 80% of the original Palestine. Despite what the Palestinians say, Israel did not usurp all of Palestine, nor are the Arabs left without a Palestinian state.

Despite the fact that all of Jordan is Palestine too, under the Oslo Accords, Israel agreed to give territorial concessions west of the Jordan River to the Palestinian Liberation Organization, (PLO) under the auspices of the Palestinian Authority (PA), whose leader is Yasser Arafat. The Jordanians have given no land into the deal.

Currently, the disputed West Bank and Gaza territory is divided into three areas, Areas A, B, and C. In Area A, which has already been given to the Palestinian Authority, the PA is in total control of the population. Under Area B, Israel is in security control, while the PA has civil authority. Area C will continue to be under Israeli security control due to its Jewish populations. These areas are redefined as land transfers made by Israel to the PA.

A "Palestinian State" does exist in Jordan with a Palestinian population. New areas have been transferred by Israel from territory west of the Jordan River. Yet, this is not enough. The Palestinians want more.

A final note on Palestine: Palestine was never a sovereign state that was somehow eclipsed in war and thus need to be re-instated back into the family of nations. What the Palestinians are asking for is the creation of an entirely new national entity.

Palestine was a regional name that was imposed on the area by the Roman Emperor, Hadrian, who supressed the Second Jewish Revolt in AD 135. He was so angry with the Jews that he wanted to humiliate them and emphasize that the Jewish nation had lost its right to a homeland under Roman rule. The name *Palaestina* was originally an adjective derived from *Philistia*, the arch-enemies of the Israelites, 1000 years earlier. Hadrian also changed the name of Jerusalem to *Aelia Capitolina* after his own family name, *Aelia*. He also forbade Jews from entering the city, except on the 9th of the Hebrew month, Av, to mourn its destruction. Since he was considered a god in the Roman Empire, this was his attempt to disconnect God's covenant between the Jewish people and their land. This effectively declared his pagan authority over Jerusalem, which had been the place of the presence of the God of Israel. To this day, Palestine flies in the face of Israel and the entire issue can be boiled down to a religious (spiritual) battle over a land whose fate

Map 8: *As you can see, the geographical facts of relinquishing the West Bank and Gaza to the PA are astonishing, as it puts the terrorist enclaves in close proximity to Jewish population centers. The major cities of Israel then fall within range of the simplest hand held rocket technology. At this point Israel becomes almost indefensible.*

will be decided by the God of the Bible, since it is His land (Lev. 25:23).

In Luke 21:24, Jesus says *"Jerusalem will be trampled on by the Gentiles until the times of the Gentiles are fulfilled."* However, just before His coming again, Jerusalem would be reunited under Jewish sovereignity, as is the case today. Israel, not Palestine, is talked about in The New Testament, with a Jewish capital, not a gentile, Moslem capital.

THE BATTLE FOR JERUSALEM

In violation of the Oslo Accords, Yasser Arafat has declared over and over again that he wants Areas B and C completely under his control, and that he is going to declare a sovereign Palestinian State, and make Jerusalem his capital. He says he will raise the Palestinian flag on the walls of the Old City of Jerusalem and on the tops of the mosques and churches.

Israel has already made a united Jerusalem its undivided capital and will not compromise on this. Therefore, if Arafat persists in pursuing his declared plan, then a war is inevitable. This is because many nations will ratify Arafat's declaration, while Israel will reject it. At this point, Jerusalem will become a flash point that will divide the nations.

Zechariah 12:2-3 states, *"Behold, I will make Jerusalem a cup of trembling unto all people round about, when they will be in siege both against Judah and against Jerusalem. And in that day I will make Jerusalem a burdensome stone of all people; and all that burden themselves with it will be cut in pieces, even though all the nations of the earth be gathered together against it."*

As believers in the Bible, we need to be sure that we are found on God's side in this issue when the inevitable battle over Jerusalem occurs. We should also write our government leaders and implore them to stand in support of Israel. Those countries, that try and divide Jerusalem and come against God's plans for that city as we prepare for the coming of Messiah, will be found fighting against God Himself.

PARTICIPATE IN GOD'S PLAN

Meanwhile, God's prophetic plan for Israel continues to progress as the land is developed, the ancient ruins are rebuilt, the fields abound with fresh fruits and vegetables, and God's ancient people continue to return.

The most recent Aliyah started in 1990 when God fulfilled Isaiah 43:5,6, which says, *"Do not be afraid, for I am with you; I will bring your children from the east and gather you from the west. I will say to the north, 'Give them up!' and to the south, 'Do not hold them back.' Bring my sons from afar and my daughters from the ends of the earth."*

In 1990-91, the Iron Curtain of Communism in the north crumbled and Jews began to pour into Israel - over 700,000 to date. From the south, the Jews of Ethiopia left their mountain villages to go "home" to Zion, and when they arrived at the airport in Addis Ababa, the Marxist government held them back for over one year. Miraculously, that government was overthrown and in the confusion, Israel was able to send more than 35 planes of every type to transport over 15,000 Ethiopian Jews to Israel in one day. God said to the south, *"Hold not back,"* and when He speaks, the miraculous occurs.

The Bible states clearly that non-Jews will participate in this great prophetic move to Zion. *"This is what the Sovereign Lord says: 'See, I will beckon to the Gentiles, I will lift up My banner to the people; they will bring your sons in their arms and carry your daughters on their shoulders."* (Isa. 49:22) *"Foreigners will rebuild your wall, and their kings will serve you. Though in anger I struck you, in favor I will show you compassion. Your gates will always stand open, they will never be shut, day or night, so that men may bring you the wealth of the nations..."* (Isa. 60:10-11).

We are called to be watchmen on the walls of Jerusalem. Isaiah 62:6,7 reminds all people who pray to the God of the Bible to *"be not silent and give God no rest until He makes Jerusalem a praise in the earth."*

Yes, God is in control and His Word will be fulfilled. *"He that keepeth Israel will not slumber nor sleep"* (Ps. 121:4).

Let us be participants with God in this prophetic move.

Let us pray for Israel and for the peace of Jerusalem. Only God's peace will be a lasting peace.

Let us also give gifts to help those returning to Zion and bless the restoration of the land of Israel.

Let us volunteer our time, if we are able.

And let us travel to Zion ourselves to see what God is doing TODAY!

For further information on this period of history, you can see the video movie, *Lawrence of Arabia*, and read the book, *The Haj*, by Leon Uris.

This Lesson from the Land of the Bible is found in our
Jerusalem Mosaic Video Series, Program #103,
along with other exciting features.
Please turn to page 186 to order your copy.

THE TRUMPET IS SOUNDING IN ZION!

Chapter 13

I have lived in Jerusalem for over 20 years, and I still get excited when I realize how privileged I am to live in this special city.

The Psalmist's description of Jerusalem as "a city compact together" aptly describes the physical appearance of Jerusalem even today...almost 3,000 years after the psalm was written. Looking at the Old City from a distance, it becomes a two-dimensional patchwork of shapes, as one building intertwines and is stacked upon another.

Not only is Jerusalem a patchwork of buildings from different historical periods, but of people, both residents and visitors alike. Here you can see Christian pilgrims from far-off lands of the world; hassidic Jews in their black tunics and knickers, fur hats and side curls; and even a Bedouin from the desert riding into town on his camel to buy supplies.

Jerusalem has been the main objective of pilgrimages of devout men and women of faith for 3,000 years. Many pilgrims have followed God's command to His people to "go up" to Jerusalem to celebrate the biblical feasts. This is critical, as He

Pilgrims came to Jerusalem to celebrate.

is reminding them, through the rituals of the feasts, of what He has done for them (and us) throughout history.

A TIME OF EXCITEMENT

The biblical festivals are an exciting time in Israel. The practice of each biblical holiday is described by the Lord in Leviticus 23 and is a part

133

of everyday life here in the land of the Bible.

The fall festivals begin with the traditional eating of apples and honey, along with festive wishes of a sweet new year on *Rosh HaShana* (literally meaning, head or beginning of the year). This holiday is also called the Feast of Trumpets because of the blowing of the trumpet *(shofar)*, calling the people to repentance and heralding in the Ten Days of Awe. This period concludes with the awesome Day of Atonement *(Yom Kippur)* with its 24-hours of strict fasting (from food and water), confession and prayer for God's forgiveness.

After the fasting on the Day of Atonement is ended, there is the excitement of building and decorating small booths, called *sukkot* or tabernacles, in preparation for the week-long Feast of Sukkot. Families eat, and some even sleep in these booths during the festival, in accordance with God's commandment to dwell in them as a reminder of their sojourning in the desert with the Lord. This week-long holiday is to be a great season of rejoicing before the Lord, ending with the joyous festival of *Simchat Torah* (meaning, the joy of God's Word) expressed with dancing and rejoicing around the Torah (the first five books of the Bible). On this day, the yearly Torah reading cycle is completed and a new one begins.

COMPLETION - A CENTRAL THEME

Interestingly, even the number of Israel's biblical festivals conveys the idea of completion. My colleague, Jim Gerrish, points out that when we add the three major festivals, *Pesach* (Passover), *Shavuot* (Pentecost) and *Sukkot* (Tabernacles), to the minor festivals associated with them, we get seven in all. Seven is the biblical number of perfection or completion.

Also, it is significant that the festivals conclude in the fall with *Sukkot*, also known as Tabernacles. The festival of *Sukkot* lasts for seven days and ends on the 21st day (3X7) of the Hebrew month of Tishri, which is Israel's seventh month.

Looking at the biblical festivals together as a complete pattern, you see a model for world history that tells us that God is soon to bring history to a conclusion.

When the trumpet of the first fall festival, *Rosh HaShana*, pierces the air, it is a reminder that both history and time are drawing to an end. Nations and individuals will eventually have their rendezvous with Jerusalem and her God (Zech. 14:16). The time for these events, that parallel the fall festival cycle, is fast approaching, just as the spring festival cycle found its fulfillment, for Christians, during the time of Yeshua (Jesus).

GOD'S SALVATION PICTURED

Christians are now beginning to realize that God's whole redemption story is pictured for us in Israel's festivals. Passover pictures salvation or deliverance from Egypt (flesh or sin). Its related festivals of Unleavened Bread and Firstfruits instruct us as to the purpose of salvation: fruitfulness in the Kingdom of God. God saves us in order that we may be holy and set apart for Him. The believing life must be a life of fruitfulness - of fruit, more fruit, even much fruit (Jn. 15:1-5). In early summer, the festival of Pentecost instructs us further concerning the kind of fruit we must bear - spiritual fruit; fruit that will last (Gal. 5:22-23). It also gives us further instruction concerning the abundance of fruit which God desires.

The Bible tells us that God, the great husbandman, eagerly awaits the precious fruit of the earth and has long patience in waiting for it (Jas. 5:7). Unfortunately, while God is focusing on fruit, we are often focusing on other things. Sometimes we even focus on gifts which God has given, instead of the fruit we are to produce as a result of God's gifts in our lives.

THE END OF THIS AGE AND THE BEGINNING OF THE NEXT

The fall festivals and the sound of the trumpet also speak to us about the end of this present evil age when so many have turned from God and His ways. For Israel and the Jewish people, the trumpet of *Rosh HaShana* was sounded to call them to repentance — those who did not repent were judged and their names were not inscribed in the Book of Life.

Soon, the trumpet will sound from Jerusalem for the whole world to come to repentance — for those who ignore it, judgment — for those who heed its call, salvation.

These fall festivals speak of a future time when men will again tabernacle with God, when He will dwell with them and they with Him (Rev. 21:3). They speak of a day in which all nations will gather to Jerusalem (Zech. 8:22; 14:16).

Interestingly, even in the days to come, Bible prophecy tells us that people from the nations of the world will come up to celebrate the Feast of Tabernacles with the Jewish people in Jerusalem (Zech. 14).

The stage is being set and prophecy is being fulfilled. The "coming-up" (*aliyah*, in Hebrew) is taking place now in Israel with the massive influx of Jews from over 100 nations. Christians, also, are already visiting the land in record numbers — the majority of pilgrims coming to Israel are Christians! We believe this is all in preparation and building for future scriptural events.

Jerusalem continues to be the focus of God's earthly pattern and plan, for ultimately it is to Jerusalem that Messiah is coming!

JERUSALEM CELEBRATES 3000 YEARS AS CAPITAL OF ISRAEL

With the sounding of the trumpet on *Rosh HaShana* in 1996, a very significant beginning to the end took place. As the Lord is setting the stage for His prophetic plan for Israel, 1996 was significant as it was the 3,000th anniversary of the establishment of Jerusalem as the capital of Israel and the Jewish people by King David in 1004 BC. Even though Jerusalem was occupied by Gentile nations since the days of the Romans, this is no longer the case.

Biblically, one of the signs that this return is soon is the fact that Jerusalem is again in the sovereign hands of the Jewish people, who have returned to their historical homeland in fulfillment of Bible prophecy. They lost this sovereignty shortly after the time of Jesus when the Romans exiled most of the Jews from the land.

However, they regained it in June 1967, when the Six Day War broke out and Jordan attacked Israel. Jerusalem was reunited under the sovereignty of the Jewish people for the first time in 1,900 years.

In Luke 21, Jesus spoke of prophetic events that would occur just before His return. Of Jerusalem, He said in verse 24, "*...and Jerusalem will be trampled on by the Gentiles until the times of the Gentiles are fulfilled.*"

Many Bible scholars believe that the reunification of Jerusalem in 1967 was a fulfillment of Luke 21:24. Is it any surprise that the sovereignty of Jerusalem is now being challenged by the Palestinian Authority, which is claiming the Old City and eastern sectors (biblical Jerusalem) as its capital, and for Islam!

In 1996, it was also 2,000 years since Yeshua (Jesus) was born in Bethlehem in 4 B.C., only a few miles south of Jerusalem.

Today, with the sound of the trumpet (on *Rosh HaShana*), all kinds of celebrations take place in Jerusalem. However, there is also great opposition to Jewish sovereignty by many nations of the world. Nevertheless, Jerusalem remains a central focus of Jews and Christians because of its centrality in the Bible.

YET, WHY JERUSALEM?

Jerusalem is just as important to God's plan now as it was then. The Bible records the event when the Lord gave Jerusalem into the hands of King David in 1,004 B.C. in I Chronicles 11:4-5,7-9:

"*David and all the Israelites marched to Jerusalem (that is, Jebus). The Jebusites who lived there said to David, 'You will not get in here.' Nevertheless, David captured the fortress of Zion, the City of David... David then took up residence in the fortress, and so it was called the City of David. He built up the city around it, from the supporting terraces to the surrounding wall, while Joab restored the rest of the city. And David became more and more powerful, because the Lord Almighty was with him.*"

David later bought the threshing floor of Araunah for an altar for the Lord (II Sam. 24) and ultimately brought the Ark of the Lord to Jerusalem (I Chron. 15). In Jerusalem, Solomon built the glorious First Temple, and it was also the site of the Second Temple, embellished to incomparable grandeur by King Herod.

Once David conquered the city, with God's blessing, the die was cast for Jerusalem to be central in world events. Jerusalem - The City of Peace. Its Hebrew name, Yerushalim ends with a plural form of shalom, the word for peace, indicating that it is not only the city of peace, but a city of a double portion of peace. Nevertheless, because God chose this city as His own, and decided that it would be the capital of Israel and the religious focal point of the Jewish people, nations have both revered and reviled this most unique city throughout history. It has been fought over by more people from more nations than any other city on earth.

Jerusalem, in the history of God's revelation and in His redemptive plan for man is, by far, the most important site on this earth:

• It was the royal city, the capital of the only kingdom God has (thus far) established among men; here the temple was erected, and here alone were sacrifices legitimately offered to the Lord.

• This was the city of the prophets, as well as the kings of David's line.

• Here occurred the death, resurrection, and ascension of *Yeshua HaMashiach*, Jesus the Messiah, and to Jerusalem He will return.

• Upon an assembled group in this city, the Holy Spirit descended at Pentecost (Shavuot), giving birth to the Church, and here the first great Church Council was held.

• Rightly, the writer of the book of Kings refers to Jerusalem as the *"city which God had chosen out of all the tribes of Israel to put His name there."*

• Even the Roman historian, Pliny, of the 1st century, referred to Jerusalem as "by far the most famous city of the ancient Orient."

• No site in all the Scriptures received such constant and exalted praise as Jerusalem. Concerning no other place in the world have such promises been made of ultimate glory and permanent peace.

• As George Adam Smith has said well, "Jerusalem felt God's presence. She was assured of His love and as never another city on earth has been, of God's travail for her worthiness of the destiny to which He had called her."

• The word Jerusalem occurs 881 times in the Bible, 667 times in the O.T. and 144 times in the N.T. In addition, the Rabbis say that there are 60 different names for Jerusalem in the Bible, with Zion being the most used name.

• Other titles for Jerusalem are: "the City of God," "The Mountain of the Lord," and numerous other references that it is His city. God Himself refers to it and to no other place, as "My City" in Isaiah 45:13, or more often, "My Holy Mountain." Because it is the City of God, where He has put His name, it is often referred to as the Holy City.

Politically, Jerusalem has been a capital city to no other nation except Israel and the Jewish people. In fact, past efforts of other nations to conquer Jerusalem have been because it was so important to the Jewish people and was the focus of their religious and political aspirations.

Geographically, it was located off the main trade routes and has no strategic importance to a conquering army other than the fact that Jerusalem was and is the God-given spiritual and administrative center of Israel.

Even Christianity and Islam centralized the importance of Jerusalem because of biblical events that were a part of the life of Israel and were later appropriated by each faith. Granted, Christianity has a direct connection to Jerusalem. However, the connection involves the life, death and resurrection of Yeshua who was Jewish, and whose mission was in context with God's redemptive plan for Israel, as well as the rest of the world.

The historical connection between the Jewish people (*Am Israel*) and Jerusalem was God's divine, covenantal, and sovereign will for this special city.

Since 1967, with Israeli sovereignty over all of Jerusalem, including the Temple Mount and the biblical Old City, we can actually celebrate the fulfillment of God's prophetic plan for Jerusalem as He sets the stage for the coming of Messiah.

You would think that the nations of the world would be rejoicing that God is fulfilling His prophetic plans for Jerusalem. But this is not so! While artists, musicians, actors, writers and a host of ordinary pilgrims visit the city to show their solidarity with Israel, the politicians of the world avoid any such support of Jerusalem as the capital of Israel. Even US presidents, who pledge to move the US Embassy from Tel Aviv to Jerusalem as a campaign platform, always renege on this pledge and vow to veto any US Congress initiatives to build a new embassy in Jerusalem!

Like the false mother who stood before Solomon, some world leaders would prefer to cut the city of Jerusalem in two and give half to the Palestinians, instead of upholding the historical right of the Jewish people and the nation of Israel to the undivided city God gave to them. The idea of dividing Jerusalem into two capitals was unspeakable only a few years ago. Now, the politicians and journalists are concerning themselves with the questions of "when," not the question of "if."

MAN DIDN'T CHOOSE JERUSALEM, GOD DID!

Yet, God will have the last word upon the nations of the world who do not uphold His prophetic will for Jerusalem.

In Isaiah 34, we find God speaking out in judgment against the nations, *"For the Lord has a day of vengeance, a year of retribution, to uphold Zion's cause."* (Isa. 34:8). The King James Version of the Bible speaks of God judging the nations *"for the controversy of Zion."*

The prophets also foretold of the centrality of Jerusalem at the end of days, when the eyes of the world would be focused on this city. Today, there is almost daily press reporting about this tiny nation. In Jerusalem, even an off-handed comment by a politician or the building of a residential neighborhood can become the stuff of a UN Security Council debate.

Of all the groups living in Jerusalem, since 1818 the Jewish population has been in the majority. Today, over 70% of Jerusalem's 600,000 residents are Jewish. Jerusalem, a dusty forgotten city with less than 15,000 inhabitants at the beginning of the 1800s, is once again the focus of the world's attention.

Psalms 102:13,14 says, *"You will arise and have compassion on Zion, for it is time to show favor to her; the appointed time has come... for her stones are dear to Your servants, her very dust moves them..."*

Since the city has been reunited, an unparalleled renovation effort has been underway by the Jewish people to restore the city to its former glory as the capital of the nation of Israel.

They have even removed the dust from the ancient stones as the archaeologists have uncovered evidence of Jerusalem's glorious past.

Yes, the time to favor Zion is now.

Many Christians and Jews alike see the restoration of Jerusalem into the hands of the Jewish people as a fulfillment of Bible prophecy. However, most people around the world see this same event as a political hot-potato.

Yet, God will have the last word upon the nations of the world who don't support His prophetic plan for Jerusalem.

In Zechariah 12, God foretold a day of judgment against the nations who come against Jerusalem, just before the coming of Messiah. Listen to what He says:

"I am going to make Jerusalem a cup that sends all the surrounding peoples reeling. Judah will be besieged as well as Jerusalem. On that day, when all the nations of the earth are gathered against her, I will make Jerusalem an immovable rock for all the nations. All who try to move it will injure themselves. On that day I will set out to destroy all the nations that attack Jerusalem" (Zech. 12:2,3,9).

Just as God used Jerusalem and Israel as a standard in days of old to determine if nations understood and supported His agenda for the world, today He is again using a regathered Israel and the city of Jerusalem, now the capital of a re-established Jewish state, as a prophetic test. Sadly, most world leaders are more intent on gaining increased influence, power and wealth as part of a New World Order, and are distancing themselves from what they see as "outdated" Bible passages and promises.

THE TRUMPET IS AGAIN SOUNDING IN JERUSALEM

God's call to all people and nations to follow Him and His eternal program may soon end abruptly in judgment upon those who choose to ignore it. We are in the season of repentance — returning to God. Regardless of the efforts of the nations of the world and the New World Order to dislocate Israel's covenantal, God-given right to this city, Bible-believers need to maintain their own strong stand in opposition to this effort. Granted, you won't be very popular for this stand, but no one who has stood boldly for biblical positions has been very popular in our world system.

Rest assured, those who oppose God's clarion call to repentance, including their attitude towards the Jewish people and the city of Jerusalem in these last days, will be judged by the Lord. It is much more than a political gesture. For the nations, it is an indication of how spiritually in tune they are to the Word of God. He has a prophetic plan that He is bringing to fulfillment.

Regardless of the efforts to re-divide Jerusalem, we need to maintain our own strong stand in favor of God's prophetic plan to prepare this city for the coming of Messiah. Naturally, we can expect the world to oppose this.

The trumpet is again sounding in Jerusalem. It is a call to get our spiritual house in order. It is also a call for Jerusalem. As the nations draw the battle lines, let us stand in support, and in prayer for the people and nation of Israel with Jerusalem as her capital. It is to Jerusalem that Messiah comes. May we all be ready!

What can we do?

In Psalm 122:6, we are called to *"Pray for the peace of Jerusalem,"* recognizing that what we are praying for is God's peace that will come according to His plan. Lydia Prince, in her book "Appointment in Jerusalem," saw the earth with one God-appointed center: JERUSALEM. Out from its center in divine plan, truth and peace were to flow to all lands; to it would return the worship and offerings of the nations. The outworking of prayer for Jerusalem would bless all lands and all peoples. Actually, the peace of the whole world depends upon the peace of Jerusalem. In the fulfillment of this plan lies earth's only hope.

Also, each of us is called to be a watchman on the walls of Jerusalem. Isaiah 62:1,6,7 reminds all people who pray to the God of the Bible, the Lord God of Israel, to continually intercede for Zion.

"For Zion's sake I will not hold my peace, and for Jerusalem's sake I will not rest, until her righteousness goes forth as brightness, and her salvation as a lamp that burns... I have set watchmen upon your walls, O Jerusalem, who will never hold their peace day nor night; you that pray to the Lord, keep not silence, and give Him no rest, until He establishes, and until He makes Jerusalem a praise in the earth" (Isa. 62:1,6,7).

Yes, Jerusalem is the City of God, and she will only find her true peace and be a praise in the earth as His prophetic Word is fulfilled.

This Lesson from the Land of the Bible is found in our
Jerusalem Mosaic Video Series, Program #107,
along with other exciting features.
Please turn to page 186 to order your copy.

Part III

Christian-Jewish Understanding

"They are beloved for the sakes of the patriarchs, for God's gifts and His call are irrevocable . . . [and that] by mercy, they shall receive mercy" (Rom. 11:28b, 11:31b).

Christian-Jewish Understanding

Warning! Do not read this chapter unless you are prepared to come face to face with the fact the many Christians and much of Christianity persecuted, exiled and even killed the Jewish people in every century since the days of Jesus.

As a Christian, I am an enthusiastic part of the Church. I desire for it to express the full message of God's love to the world. However, Christianity has not always done this and has often failed in its mission. Much of what you will read about Church relations with the Jewish people will disturb you. Yet, it should not shake your faith in the Lord or your commitment to stand with the Church. Our spiritual foundation of faith should always be in the Lord of the Church, not the Church as an institution. Why? The Church is run by people, and people are fallible and make mistakes. The Lord is head of the Church, but the leaders and congregants are not always listening and carrying out His Word.

That is what happened in relation to the Jewish people. The Church failed the Jewish people because they did not live out God's Word in their relationship with them. Horrible mistakes were made. While we cannot change the past, we can change the future. George Santayana said, "Those who cannot remember the past are condemned to repeat it."

Therefore, this lesson is not written to cast stones at Christianity or past leaders of the Church. Rather, it is to learn from the mistakes that were made so that we won't repeat them. This lesson will also allow us to see Christianity as the Jewish people have seen it for the past 2,000 years. Then, we will understand why they are often very afraid of Christians, even of those who are trying to build positive relationships. After 2,000 years of Christian hatred and persecution, they don't understand the change of heart of many Christians today, or don't believe it is real.

This is not just a history lesson, but an opportunity to soften our hearts towards Israel and the Jewish people and create within each of us a desire to deliver the correct message of Christianity. It is exciting to see Christians today re-grafting into the tree of Israel, according to God's plan in Romans 11. When we live unattached from the root of Israel, we are like a beautiful bouquet of cut flowers... we flourish for a short time and then wither apart from our roots. That is the picture of much of Church history. On the other hand, reattached to our spiritual, Hebraic Old Testament roots, we will drink in new life and understanding that will make our New Testament faith come alive.

It was never God's intention that there would be a separation between His Church and Israel. Jesus was to be the One to break down the middle wall of partition and make of two, one new man (Eph. 2:14-18). Paul teaches us that it is by our mercy that they (the Jewish people) would receive God's mercy (Rom. 11:31).

Please read this message, "Where Was Love and Mercy?", with an open heart. May it inspire you to change history and show God's love and mercy to Israel and the Jewish people.

WHERE WAS LOVE & MERCY?

THE HISTORY OF CHRISTIAN ANTI-SEMITISM

Chapter 14

- Did you know that the early Church was predominantly Jewish?
- What happened to disconnect the Church from its Jewish roots and create an almost entirely Gentile Church?
- Why did the Church enact so many anti-Jewish edicts?
- Are the Jewish people "Christ killers," as they have been called in Christian circles?
- Has the Church replaced Israel?
- Why did historical events like the Cru sades and the Inquisition ultimately focus on persecuting Jews?
- Did you know that Martin Luther had a very positive relationship with the Jewish community, and then became one of the vilest anti-Semites in history?
- Did you know that Adolph Hitler found precedent for his evil actions against the Jewish people right out of the annals of Church history?
- What can we do to change the last 1,800 years of historical anti-Jewish attitudes and actions of the Church?

Early Church Father

We Christians sing the chorus, *"They will know we are Christians, by our love, by our love...."* In Romans 11, Paul tells Gentile Christians of our relationship towards the Jewish people. He tells us not to be *"arrogant"* towards them (v. 20), that they are *"beloved for the sake of the Patriarchs"* (v. 28) and that *"through [our] mercy, they shall obtain mercy"* (v. 31). Sadly, the Jewish community, living in close proximity to Christians throughout the last 1,900 years, has rarely felt any love or respect from Christians or Christianity. For the most part, they received hatred, contempt, persecution, and even death at the hands of Christians. Where was love and mercy?

Generally, very little of this very vivid and tragic history is known to most Christians. Yet, it is well-known by the Jewish community, because they remember these sad chapters of history all too well. Instead of showing love and mercy to the Jewish people, many Christians turned the cross into a sword against the Jews. It has been said by Dr. Edward Flannery, in his book, *The Anguish of the Jews,* that the only chapters of Christian history known by the Jews were recorded on pages the Church has torn out of the history books and burned. In researching this article, I checked volume after volume of books, encyclopedias and dictionaries of Church History, and there was barely a reference to be found about the large quantity of material written by the Church against the Jewish people. They exist as part of the proceedings and conclusions of most Church Councils and Edicts up until this century, but most writers preferred not to write about these passages because it was not flattering. Rather, we have simply swept it under the carpet because it is all too uncomfortable to deal with.

This is why I want us to do something a little different in this chapter. Instead of looking at a right understanding and interpretation of Scripture, we are going to see the results of wrong interpretation and the havoc it wreaked. Because this is so central to our Christian relationship to Israel and the Jewish community, it is very important to study this together. While it is a lengthy topic, I assure you that you will not be bored.

When we examine the last 2,000 years in historical perspective, I feel it is safe to say that organizations and individual Christians who express Christian solidarity with the Jewish people, and are educating the Church about the Jewish roots of the Christian faith, are a historical rarity.

Let me put this assessment in perspective: During approximately 1,800 years of the nearly 2,000 years of Church history, any attempt to teach Christians about Jews, Judaism, Jewish roots of Christianity, or even to celebrate the Levitical Feasts, would result in Christians being subject to a good tongue-lashing or excommunication at best, and in many cases, death. And, any member of the Jewish community participating would be considered Judaisers and penalized by Church authorities with punishment and even death. Certainly an article of this kind was not allowed. While history is complex (and there were certain historical moments of religious freedom), this assessment can be considered an accurate generalization.

Fortunately today, we are free to discuss the Jewish roots of Christianity, as well as our own sad record against the Jews, without retribution. We can even come together with Jews to learn from one another on these topics. The trend is definitely positive.

This study is not intended to be a mere history lesson, but a lesson in history. Furthermore, I am not trying to impose guilt on anyone, for we are exceptions to the historical rule. On the other hand, I am trying to instill a sense of responsibility, so that we will not allow history to repeat itself.

In this presentation, I will be referring to early Church Fathers, the Catholic Church, Martin Luther, and other Church leaders and Church edicts. Please don't be offended by the historical facts presented. They are being presented to help us to learn, grow, and move ahead in our faith walk, not to insult any particular denomination or group. So, let's get started on our journey into understanding.

THE FIRST FOUR CENTURIES A.D.

In the first century AD, the church was well-connected to its Jewish roots, and Jesus did not intend for it to be any other way. After all, Jesus is Jewish and the basis of His teaching is consistent with the Hebrew Scriptures. In Matthew 5:17-18 He states: *"Do not think that I have come to abolish the Law or the Prophets; I have not come to abolish them but to fulfil them. I tell you the truth, until heaven and earth disappear, not the smallest letter, not the least stroke of a pen, will by any means disappear from the Law until everything is accomplished."*

Jesus is Jewish and the basis of His teaching is consistent with the Hebrew Scriptures.

It is also known that the writers of the New Testament, except Luke, were Jewish. The apostles and early disciples were Jewish. They worshipped on *Shabbat* (Sabbath), celebrated the feasts, and attended Synagogue. Even the membership of the early Church in Jerusalem and surrounding Judea, Samaria, and Galilee was predominately Jewish. We know, for example, that no non-Jewish names appeared in leadership of the Jerusalem church until after AD 135, when a Greek name appears. We will see why this happened in a moment.

Congregations in other parts of the Roman Empire also had relatively strong Jewish or Hebraic roots, as they found their source of guidance from the Jerusalem School of Thought. This is illustrated by the names of many of the New Testament epistles: The Letters *TO* the Corinthians, Romans, Galatians, Ephesians, Philippians, Colossians, and Thessalonians, originated from the Jerusalem community. The writers of the other Epistles were also connected to the Judeo-Christian congregation in Jerusalem.

Before the First Jewish Revolt in AD 66, Christianity was basically a sect of Judaism, as were the Pharisees, Sadducees, and Essenes. The Christians were also known as Nazarenes. Before the First Jewish Revolt that ended with the Second Temple being destroyed and Jerusalem razed by the Romans in AD 70, there was room for debate within Judaism in the bustling, cosmopolitan city of Jerusalem. So, what happened to cause such a split between the Christian and Jewish communities that exists even unto today?

The Separation Begins: Initially, it began as a result of religious and social differences. According to David Rausch in his book, *A Legacy of Hatred*, there were several contributing factors: 1) the Roman intrusion into Judea, and the widespread acceptance of Christianity by the Gentiles, complicated the history of Jewish Christianity; 2) the Roman wars against the Jews not only destroyed the Temple and Jerusalem, but also resulted in Jerusalem's relinquishing her position as a center of Christian faith in the Roman world; and, 3) the rapid acceptance of Christianity among the Gentiles led to an early conflict between the Church and Synagogue. Paul's missionary journeys brought the Christian faith to the Gentile world, and as their numbers grew, so did their influence, which ultimately disconnected Christianity from its Jewish roots.

Many Gentile Christians interpreted the destruction of the Temple and Jerusalem as a sign that God had abandoned Judaism, and that He had provided the Gentiles freedom to develop their own Christian theology in a setting free from Jerusalem's influence. Unfortunately, the Judeo-Christians had disassociated themselves from the war against the Romans and from the tragedy that had come upon the nation. Believing that the war with the Romans was a sign of the end, they fled to Pella, east of the Jordan River, leaving their fellow Jews to fend for themselves.

After the war and the virtual destruction of Jerusalem and the Temple, the Jewish sages who managed to survive the Roman victory assembled in Jabneh, a city in the Sharon Plains near Joppa. As they entered the post-Temple period, they realized the need to consolidate the practice of Judaism and *halacha,* or Law. Judaism adopted the Bet Hillel School of rabbinical practice, which was most closely linked to the Pharisaic sect of Judaism. The Pharisaic teachings were most interested in the relationship of each individual to God, and encouraged the masses to holiness based on a scrupulous observance of the Torah, unlike Sadducean teaching that was more interested in Temple ritual practice. Even though Pharisaic Judaism had shown tolerance to Judeo-Christians or Nazarenes prior to the destruction of the Temple, the assembly at Jabneh called for a separation between Christianity and Judaism.

Hadrian's Contribution: In AD 132, when the Jewish zealot, Bar Kochba, orchestrated the Second Jewish Revolt against Rome, the Judeo-Christians had another reason not to participate. Bar Kochba was proclaimed the Messiah by Rabbi Akiva. Since the Christians saw Jesus (Yeshua) as Messiah, for them to participate in the revolt under the leadership of Bar Kochba would be considered a denial of their beliefs. In AD 135, when the revolt was crushed by the Roman Emperor Hadrian, he expelled all Jews from Jerusalem, allowing them to return only one day each year, on *Tisha B'Av,* an annual day set aside to mourn

Hadrian pictured on coin which depicts Judea as a woman.

the destruction of the Temple. This prohibition was also true for Judeo-Christians, and thus we find recorded the first Greek name in the leadership of the Jerusalem Church. At this point, the Hebraic influence of the Jerusalem Church was lost to world Christianity, which influenced the direction of the Church.

Hadrian also rebuilt Jerusalem into a Roman city, naming it after himself, *Aelia Capitolina*, his family name being Aelius. As one considered a god by his subjects, this was a supreme insult to the God of Israel who chose Jerusalem as His city. Hadrian also changed the name of Judea, Samaria and Galilee to *Syria Palestina* (Palestine), ascribing to the land a name connected to the arch-enemies of the Jewish people, the Philistines. Both gestures were done by Hadrian to erase any Jewish connection with the city of Jerusalem and the land of Israel. This legacy is still haunting Israel today.

Christianity and Judaism Separate: By this time, the Church had effectively separated itself from Judaism. Theological and political power moved from Jewish Christian leaders to centers of Gentile Christian leadership such as Alexandria, Rome, and Antioch. It is important to understand this change, because it influenced the early Church Fathers to make anti-Jewish statements as Christianity began to disconnect itself from its Jewish roots.

As the Church spread far and wide within the Roman Empire, and its membership grew increasingly non-Jewish, Greek and Roman thought began to creep in and completely change the orientation of Biblical interpretation through a Greek mindset,

Mosaic showing Christian woman being thrown alive to the lions, from a villa in Carthage.

rather than a Jewish or Hebraic mindset. This would later result in many heresies, some of which the Church is still practicing today.

Once Christianity and Judaism began to take separate paths, the void became greater and greater. The Romans had effectively suppressed Judaism; however, Christianity was spreading quickly. This became a major concern to Rome, and ultimately political pressure became a major factor in the widening rift between Christians and Jews.

Under Roman law, Judaism was considered a *religio licita*, a legal religion, as it predated Rome. To unify the Roman Empire, everyone was to worship and sacrifice to the Roman gods, which included the Emperor who was considered a god. Obviously, the Christians could not ascribe to this pagan worship and refused, angering the central Roman authority. Christianity post-dated Rome, and therefore was considered a *religio ilicita*. The practice of Christianity was a punishable offense. During this time, we find Christians being used for sport in the Roman coliseums and circuses, as gladiators or thrown to the lions and other wild beasts. The Emperor Nero even used Christians as human torches to light up his gardens at night. Christians were dipped in pitch, tied to poles and set afire. For protection against arrest, the symbol of the fish, rather than the obvious symbol of the cross, was used between Christians as a sign of identification during this period. The Greek anagram of the slogan, "Jesus Christ, Son of God, Savior" spelled the word, ICTHUS, or fish in Greek.

In an attempt to alleviate this persecution, Christian apologists tried in vain to convince Rome that Christianity was an extension of Judaism. However, Rome was not convinced. The resulting persecutions and frustration of the Christians bred an animosity towards the Jewish community, which was free to worship without persecution. Later, when the Church became the religion of the state, it would pass laws against the Jews in retribution.

Replacement Theology: This animosity was reflected in the writings of the early Church Fathers. For example, Justin Martyr (c. AD 160) in speaking to a Jew said: "The Scriptures are not yours, but ours." Irenaeus, Bishop of Lyon (c. AD 177) declared: "Jews are disinherited from the grace of God." Tertullian (AD 160-230), in his treatise, *"Against the Jews,"* announced that God had rejected the Jews in favor of the Christians.

In the early 4th century, Eusebius wrote that the promises of the Hebrew Scriptures were for Christians and not the Jews, and the curses were for the Jews. He argued that the Church was the continuation of the Old Testament and thus superseded Judaism. The young Church declared itself to be the true Israel, or "Israel according to the Spirit," heir to the divine promises. They found it essential to discredit the "Israel according to the flesh" to prove that God had cast away His people and transferred His love to the Christians.

In this, we find the beginnings of Replacement Theology, which placed the Church Triumphant over the vanquished Judaism and Israel. This Replacement theory became one of the main foundations on which Christian anti-Semitism was based, even to this day. Incidentally, the New Testament speaks of the Church's relationship to Israel and her covenants as being *"grafted in"* (Rom. 11:17), *"brought near"* (Eph. 2:13), *"Abraham's offspring* (by faith)" (Rom. 4:16), and *"partakers"* (Rom. 15:27), NOT as usurpers of the covenant and a replacer of physical Israel. We Gentile Christians joined into what God had been doing in Israel, and God did not break His covenant promises with Israel (Rom. 11:29).

The Church Triumphant: At the beginning of the 4th century, a monumental event occurred for the Church. In AD 306, Constantine became the first Christian Roman Emperor. At first, he had a rather pluralistic view and accorded Jews the same religious rights as Christians. However, in AD 321, he made Christianity the official religion of the Empire. This signaled the end of the persecution of Christians, but the beginning of discrimination and persecution of the Jewish people.

Already at a council in Elvira (Spain) in AD 305, declarations were made to keep Jews and Christians apart, including ordering Christians not to share meals with Jews, not to marry Jews, not to use Jews to bless their fields, and not to observe the Jewish Sabbath.

Imperial Rome, in AD 313, issued the Edict of Milan, which granted favor to Christianity, while outlawing synagogues. Then, in AD 315, another edict allowed the burning of Jews if they were convicted of breaking the laws. As Christianity was becoming the religion of the state, further laws were passed against the Jews:

- The ancient privileges granted to the
  Jews were withdrawn.
- Rabbinical jurisdiction was
  abolished or severely curtailed.
- Proselytism was prohibited and
  made punishable by death.
- Jews were excluded from holding high office
  or a military career.

These and other restrictions were confirmed over and over again by various Church Councils for the next 1,000 years.

In AD 321, Constantine decreed all business should cease on "the honored day of the sun." By substituting Sunday for Saturday as the day for Christian worship, he further advanced the split. This Jewish Shabbat/ Christian Sunday controversy also came up at the first real ecumenical Council of Nicea (AD 325), which concluded Sunday to be the Christian day of rest, although it was debated for long after that.

Overnight, Christianity was given the power of the Imperial State, and the emperors began to translate the concepts and claims of the Christian theologians against the Jews and Judaism into practice. Instead of the Church taking this opportunity to spread its Gospel message in love, it truly became the Church Triumphant, ready to vanquish its foes. After 321, the writings of the Church Fathers changed in character. No longer was it on the defensive and apologetic, but aggressive, directing its venom at everyone "outside of the flock," in particular the Jewish people who could be found in almost every community and nation.

THE MIDDLE AGES

Now let's look at the next 700 years of history, from the time of Constantine to the First Crusade in AD 1096.

This period is known as the Middle Ages, or Dark Ages. The Holy Roman Empire was seeking to expand the new faith in the pagan tribes of Western Europe, the Ostrogoths in the north and east, the Visigoths in the West, and the Frankish Empire which included an area roughly surrounding France today.

During this period, we find more examples of anti-Jewish bias in Church literature written by church leaders:

- Hilary of Poitiers (AD 291-371) wrote: "Jews are a perverse people accursed by God forever."
- Gregory of Hyssa (died AD 394), Bishop of Cappadocia: "the Jews are a brood of vipers, haters of goodness..."
- St. Jerome (AD 347-407) describes the Jews as "... serpents, wearing the image of Judas, their psalms and prayers are the braying of donkeys."

John Chrysostom: At the end of the 4th century, the Bishop of Antioch, John Chrysostom, the great orator, wrote a series of eight sermons against the Jews. He had seen Christians talking with Jewish people, taking oaths in front of the Ark, and some were keeping the Jewish feasts. He wanted this to stop. In an effort to bring his people back to what

he called, "the true faith," the Jews became the whipping boy for his sermon series. To quote him, "the synagogue is not only a brothel and a theater; it is also a den of robbers and a lodging for wild beasts. No Jew adores God... Jews are inveterate murderers, possessed by the devil, their debauchery and drunkenness gives them the manners of the pig. They kill and maim one another..."

One can easily see that a Judeo-Christian who wanted to hold on to his heritage, or a Gentile Christian who wanted to learn more about the parent of Christianity, would have found it extremely difficult under this pressure. Further,

John Chrysostom

Chrysostom sought to separate Christianity totally from Judaism. He wrote in his 4th Discourse, "I have said enough against those who say they are on our side, but are eager to follow the Jewish rites... it is against the Jews that I wish to draw up my battle... Jews are abandoned by God and for the crime of deicide, there is no expiation possible."

Chrysostom was known for his fiery preaching against what he saw as threats to his flock, including wealth, entertainment, privilege and outward adornment. However, his preaching against the Jewish community, which he believed had a negative influence on Christians, is inexcusable and blatantly anti-Semitic in its content.

The Christ Killers: Another unfortunate contribution Chrysostom made to Christian anti-Semitism was to hold the whole Jewish people culpable for the killing of Christ. The label of "Christ-killers," as applied to the Jewish people, was to be reaffirmed by anti-Semites for the next 16 centuries.

Let's look at this issue for a moment and squash it once and for all. To justify this label of "Christ-killer," Matthew 27:25 has been cited. In this passage, the Jewish people are shown admitting their collective responsibility for the crucifixion of Jesus, *"Then answered all the people and said, 'His blood be upon us, and our children.'"*

First, the collective responsibility of an entire people for all generations cannot be validated by the words of a few. They were speaking for themselves, not all Israel or all the Jewish people.

Secondly, if they were held responsible for the death of Jesus for their participation, then the non-Jewish world is also guilty of the same responsibility because it was Roman Gentile soldiers who actually carried out the crucifixion and drove the nails into Jesus and hung Him on the cross. Well, if not all Gentiles, at least we can hold it against all Italians!! I think you can see how ludicrous this argument is.

Ecclesia and Synagoga - a pair of statues erected in Gothic cathedrals in Europe to symbolize the Church triumphant and the Synagogue rejected and fallen. The Church is depicted as a proud, crowned, but modest maiden, while the Synagogue is depicted with broken staff, blindfolded, and holding broken tablets of the law - her crown has fallen.

Thirdly, Jesus willingly gave Himself up to die for the sins of mankind. So ultimately, it was our sin that nailed Him to the cross — not a Jewish mob, or a Roman army.

Fourthly, before Jesus died, He said, *"Father forgive them, they know not what they do"* (Lk. 23:24). If Jesus forgave both the Jewish and Roman players in this event, then who are we to do any less?

The Jews as a Witness People: Moving ahead in this period of the Middle Ages, we find some church leaders perplexed. If the Jews and Judaism were cursed by God, as they had been teaching for centuries, then how can you explain their existence?

Augustine tackled this issue in his "Sermon Against the Jews." He asserts that even though the Jews deserved the most severe punishment for having put Jesus to death, they have been kept alive by Divine Providence to serve, together with their Scriptures, as witnesses to the truth of Christianity. Their existence was further justified by the service they rendered to the Christian truth, in attesting through their humiliation, the triumph of the Church over the Synagogue. They were to be a "Witness people" - slaves and servants who should be humbled.

The monarchs of the Holy Roman Empire thus regarded the Jews as serfs of the chamber (*servi camerae*), and utilized them as slave librarians to maintain Hebrew writings. They also utilized the services of Jews in another enterprise - usury, or money-lending. The loaning of money was necessary to a growing economy. However, usury was considered to endanger the eternal salvation of the Christian, and was thus forbidden. So, the church endorsed the practice of lending by Jews, for according to their reasoning, their Jewish souls were lost in any case. Much later, the Jewish people were utilized by the Western countries as trade agents in commerce, and thus we see how the Jewish people found their way into the fields of banking and commerce.

So, by the Middle Ages, the ideological arsenal of Christian anti-Semitism was completely established. This was further manifested in a variety of precedent-setting events within the Church, such as Patriarch Cyril, Bishop of Alexandria, expelling the Jews and giving their property to a Christian mob. From a social standpoint, the deterioration of the Jewish position in society was only beginning its decline. During this early period, the virulent judeophobia was primarily limited to the clergy who were always trying to keep their flocks away from the Jews. However, later, the rank and file, growing middle class would be the main source of anti-Semitic activity.

THE CRUSADES

The First Crusade began in the year 1096. This was a period of strife for the Western Church. There were two Popes, one considered an anti-Pope who was claiming the position. When one died, the other, Urban II, needed a unifying cause. So, he called for a Crusade, or Holy War, against the Moslems in the Holy Land, who were persecuting Christians and desecrating the holy places and Jerusalem.

In the summer of 1096, an undisciplined rabble of 200,000 peas-

Even though the Crusaders initially targeted Moslems, Jews in both Europe and the Holy Land became the focus of the massacres. In this artist's depiction, the body parts of victims of the battle are thought to be Jews.

ants and artisans assembled in France. However, there were no Moslems near at hand. So the "champions of the cross" turned their attention to the Jews, who, in their eyes, were just as much "infidels" and enemies of Christianity as the Moslems. They found they could begin the Crusade on the spot. Cruelty, instead of charity, began at home.

As the Crusaders marched through Europe on their way to the Holy Land, they literally raped, pillaged and plundered the Jewish communities along the way. Faced with the wild cries of the Crusaders, "The Jews crucified our Savior, and they must return to Him or die," the Jews had the alternative of baptism or death. Thousands preferred the death of martyrs.

While the Church did not officially sanction this activity, it nevertheless took place with very little to stop it. Many local clergymen and bishops did give some Jews protection and refuge from the rabble. Unfortunately, others actually participated in the executions.

For example, at Mainz, in Germany, the Archbishop invited 1,300 Jews into his palace for refuge. This proved to be an invitation to slaughter, for under his supervision, they were all killed. He even shared in the spoils confiscated from the corpses. Incidentally, Emperor Henry IV heard of this massacre, confiscated the property of the Archbishop, and permitted the Jews who had been forcibly baptized in his realm to return to Judaism.

When the Crusaders finally arrived in Jerusalem three years later, they were 600,000 strong. They besieged the city and on July 15, 1099, broke through the walls. They killed the Moslems in the city, along with many Christians whom they mistook for Moslems because of their Middle Eastern appearance. They herded the Jews into their synagogues. Crusaders with shields decorated with large crosses placed wood around the synagogues and burned alive all inside as they sang, "Christ, We Adore Thee!"

Is it any wonder that, for the Jewish people, the cross is a symbol of hatred and death, not love, reconciliation and salvation? The cross has literally been taken and used as a sword against the Jewish people.

In all, there were nine Crusades. The last was in 1291, when the Moslems once again took possession of the Holy Land.

THE FOURTH LATERAN COUNCIL

In 1215, the Fourth Lateran Council of the Church was held. During this council, the doctrine of Transubstantiation was crystallized. Transubstantiation is the doctrine that the flesh and blood of Christ becomes present in the consecrated host (bread) and wine. This doctrine is still believed in the Catholic Church today. This doctrine, together with other statements of the Fourth Lateran Council, became a new source of Christian anti-Semitism.

1) **Host Desecration:** For centuries to follow, accusations of host desecration by Jews were circulated. The "Host Desecration Libel" is that the Jewish people would try to steal a consecrated host and then stab, torment, and burn it in an effort to recrucify Christ. Many illustrated sto-

ries showing this fabricated phenomenon were circulated, particularly in Germany, during the 1400s and 1500s. This teaching is not dead.

Let me share a personal example. In the mid-1970s, the children of a Catholic friend came home from a parochial school (in Boston, MA) with this story told them by a nun trying to teach them respect for the communion host (bread wafer): "A Catholic boy and a Jewish boy went into a Catholic church, and the Jewish boy talked the Christian boy into stealing a communion host. They took it home and went into a closet and stuck it with a pin. The host began to bleed, filled up the closet with blood, and drowned the boys!" This is a variation of the old blood libel charge, particularly since the culprit in the story is a Jew.

2) **Blood Libel:** An offshoot of the host desecration libel is the "blood libel." The blood libel contends that Jews murder non-Jews, particularly Christians, in order to obtain blood for the Passover or other rituals. It was also purported that Jews needed to drink Christian blood so that their appearance could remain human looking, and Christian blood would also help eliminate the distinctive *foetor judaicus*, "Jewish smell," which was converse to the "odor of sanctity" possessed by Christians. Another version of this accusation is that Jews would kidnap Christian babies, kill them, and grind up their bodies to cook in their matza (unleavened bread) for Passover. These libels are easily refuted when one has only the slightest understanding of Jewish dietary laws. Jewish people are forbidden to eat the blood of any animal, much less human blood or flesh. The fact that such a doctrine could come into being shows complete contempt and ignorance of Jewish lifestyle, and the lack of any Christian-Jewish relations and dialogue.

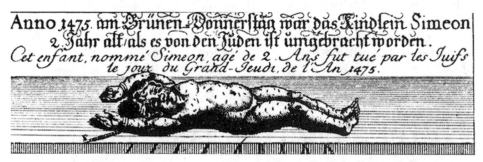

An early 18th-century Frankfort broadsheet of the Blood Libel, the accusation that Jews murdered Christian children to obtain blood for the Passover ritual.

Again, these accusations can still be found today. Not too many years ago, a young boy was kidnapped in a town north of Minneapolis. JoAnn Magnuson, our BFP Education Director in the US, has a copy of a flyer that was put on windshields in the area claiming that Jews had kidnapped the child for their Passover rituals. It sounds absurd that such a thing could be claimed in the 1990s, but anti-Semitism does not die an easy death.

3) **Distinguishing Marks:**   Another canon promulgated by the Fourth Lateran Council required Jews to wear a distinguishing mark. The form of the mark varied in different countries, but usually took the form

of a badge, or a three-cornered or pointed hat. In this way, Christians could be sure not to inadvertently come into contact with Jewish people. Even in Medieval art, Jews were depicted in paintings and woodcuts with a circle on their clothing or wearing pointed hats.

It is important to realize that during this period, many lay and ecclesiastical authorities tried to protect the Jewish community from persecution. Much of the anti-Semitism was now promoted by a rising middle-class. However, the attitudes were based on Church teaching of the past.

THE INQUISITION

The next historical event to blemish world history is the infamous Inquisition promoted by the Church in Spain and Portugal.

According to Canon Law, the Inquisition was not authorized to interfere in the internal affairs of the Jews, but to seek out Christian heretics who had backslidden. However, this law was rescinded on the grounds that the presence of Jews caused heresy to develop in the Christian communities.

In the mid-1400s, the Spanish Inquisition began to identify and prosecute backsliders in the Church. It then spread to the Jewish community. Its first focus was the tens of thousands of Jews who had been forcibly baptized. These baptized Jews were known as Conversos or New Christians. Because of this, they were considered Christians and expected to behave as Christians, even though conversion was not their choice. If a mouse is caught in a cookie jar, this does not make him a cookie. So too, force-baptizing anyone does not make him a Christian. Many of these New Christians took upon themselves a Christian facade in order to live and work in the Christian society of Spain and Portugal.

Others did not, and were persecuted for their faith. Many were still practicing Jewish customs, such as lighting candles on Friday evening, changing the linen on the Sabbath, abstaining from pork and scaleless fish, observing the Feast Days, etc. According to the Inquisition Laws, to be caught practicing any one of 37 Jewish customs was grounds to be brought before the Inquisition Court. Christians were to watch for these signs and report any such backsliders. Once before the court, there was no way out of punishment:

- If you confessed and did not repent, you were burned alive.
- If you confessed and repented, you were publicly humiliated. Any subsequent slip-ups resulted in certain death.
- If you did not confess, even if you were innocent, you were tortured until you confessed and then were burned.

The Church was not allowed to execute the victim, so they passed them to a secular arm of the Inquisition Court. Blood was not allowed to be shed, thus burning was the execution of choice. This they justified by a text from John 15:6, *"If a man abide not in Me, he is cast forth as a branch, and is withered, and men gather them, and cast them into the fire, and they are burned."*

Incidentally, all their property was confiscated, enriching the Inquisition Court.

Finally, practicing Jews (not Conversos) were eventually brought to the Inquisition Courts, as it was believed that they were Judaisers and a bad influence on the Conversos. They too were tried and burned.

The Inquisition in Spain lasted from 1481-1820. Over 350,000 Jews suffered punishment.

THE REFORMATION

Finally, we hope for a breath of fresh air. Reformers recognized many errors inherent in the Church and challenged the leadership, the Pope, the bishops, the priests — the whole ecclesiastical body. The Reformation brought about complex and even contradictory repercussions to the evolution of anti-Semitism.

One branch of Protestantism, namely the Calvinists and their offshoots, proved less judeophobic than Catholicism until the 20th century.

The other branch, Lutheranism, developed a continuing strain of anti-Semitism due to Luther's later anti-Jewish views.

An immediate consequence of the Reformation was to aggravate the position of the Jews in regions that remained Roman Catholic. The popes were determined to restore order by the strict application of Canon Law. This naturally affected the Jewish people negatively. One result was that from the second half of the 16th century, ghettos were introduced, at first in Italy, and afterward in the Austrian Empire. The ghetto was actually the name of an island in Venice that was an abandoned foundry. The Jews of Venice were rounded up and moved there so they could be separated and watched. This practice spread to other parts of the Catholic world. Adolph Hitler reinstituted the ghetto in the Third Reich for the same purpose. G. E. Roberti, an 18th century Catholic publicist, stated: "A Jewish ghetto is a better proof of the truth of the religion of Jesus Christ than a whole school of theologians."

The title page of the most virulent of Martin Luther's anti-Semitic pamphlets, "On The Jews and Their Lies."

Martin Luther: Martin Luther is the father of Lutheranism. During the first period of his ministry, 1513-1523, Luther often condemned the persecution of the Jews and recommended a more tolerant policy toward them, based on the spirit of true brotherhood. In 1523, he wrote a pamphlet, *"That Christ Was Born A Jew,"* in which he argued that the Jews, who were from the same stock as the founder of Christianity, had been right in refusing to accept the "papal paganism" presented to them as Christianity. He added, "If I had been a Jew and had seen such fools and blockheads teach the Christian faith, I should rather have turned into a pig than become a Christian."

However, when they did not accept his version of Christianity and convert, Luther turned increasingly hostile to the Jewish people. By the 1530s in his *Table Talk Series*, he referred to them as "the stiffed-necked Jews, ironhearted and stubborn as the devil."

Finally, it happened. He printed two pamphlets, in 1542, *"On the Jews and Their Lies,"* and in 1543, *"On The Shem Hamephoras"* (The Ineffable Name). These two pamphlets contain some of the most abhorrent and vile language ever written against the Jewish people.

Five hundred years later, Hitler found many of his ideas and justifications for his treatment of the Jewish people and the Holocaust in these writings. After all, if the father of the Lutheran Church, who was a German, stated these things, who was to argue with him? For Luther, it was certainly a case of "sowing the wind and reaping the whirlwind."

THE ENLIGHTENMENT AND EMANCIPATION

As we move into the era of Enlightenment in the 17th and 18th centuries, we find the Jewish people still suffering from a legacy of prejudice. As long as Christianity held unchallenged sway in Europe, Jews could exist only on the margin of European social life, and were not even allowed to own property. The term, the *Wandering Jew*, found its definition in the fact that the Jewish people were forced from city to city, and country to country. For this reason, the Jewish people gravitated to occupations of the intellect, commerce and the arts, professions they could take with them if forced to leave. Not being able to buy property, they often put their wealth into jewelry or other easily transportable commodities. This, and their vocation in banking and money lending, forced upon them by Church authorities since the 12th Century, gave them an undeserved reputation of being obsessed with money.

They became the scapegoat for the ills of the world. When the people of Europe were dying from the Black Death (Bubonic Plague), the Jews were blamed for poisoning the wells. Lacking knowledge regarding germs and disease, and seeing most of the Jewish people free from infection (which was due to their dietary habits and cleanliness), the conclusion of the non-Jewish citizens was that the Jews were the source of the problem. After all, the Jews were still being pictured as evil and prompted by the devil to do evil deeds. Or, they were caricaturized as creatures with pointed tails, horns, and devilish features.

As we move into the era of Emancipation, the newer 19th century version of anti-Semitism arose on soil, which had been well watered for many centuries in Europe by Christian theology and popular myths about the Jewish people. For centuries, Christians had persecuted Jews for theological reasons, and this "teaching of contempt" had set the seal on the most ancient of all anti-Semitic themes: that the Jews were a uniquely alien element within human society and the enemy of the modern secular state. The end of the Medieval era of faith and politics did not mean the end of anti-Semitism.

THE POGROMS OF RUSSIA

From 1881 to 1902, there was a series of pogroms against the Jews of Russia. The Pogroms were a series of attacks, accompanied by destruction, the looting of property, murder, and rape, perpetrated by the Christian population of Russia against the Jews. Civil and military authorities stood by and watched, and at times participated. The Church was silent at best, and even endorsed some of the attacks. It was during this period that we find the infamous publication, *The Protocols Of The Learned Elders Of Zion*. The Protocols, first printed in Russia in 1905, is a supposed conversation between Jewish leaders on how they were to take over the world. The original publication was printed under the auspices of the secret police on the press of Czar Nicolas II of Russia, who made no secret of his personal membership in the anti-Semitic organization, the Black Hundreds. Even though this booklet has been proven over and over again to be false, it can still be found in print around the world and in many languages.

It is difficult to assess the full scope of the pogroms and the number of victims they claimed because of a civil war affecting Russia at the turn of the century. However, partial data is available for 530 communities in which 887 major pogroms and 349 minor pogroms occurred; there were 60,000 dead and several times that number of wounded. (Dubnow, History of Russia.)

THE HOLOCAUST

This brings us to the Holocaust, the culmination of 1900 years of bad teaching in Christian society. The Holocaust was Hitler's Final Solution of the Jewish people.

Egyptian edition of "The Protocols of the Learned Elders of Zion."

Germany was one of the most enlightened, intellectual, and cultured societies in the world at that time. Yet, this so-called Christian society stood by and watched the extermination of the Jews of Europe, and some even participated.

Six million Jews including two million children were violently murdered by Hitler and the Nazis. His Final Solution was to rid the world of the "Jewish vermin," as he portrayed them in literature, speeches, and films. Hitler concluded that there was an evil in society and the common denominator was Jews who could be found in every city and in every country of Europe. To Hitler, they were an ever-present and evil burden to society. They were the killers of Christ. They needed to be controlled and segregated from the rest of society and wear distinguishing badges. They should only work in menial tasks and be barred from medicine, the arts, sciences, law, education, etc. Their synagogues and prayer books should be burned, their property confiscated, and ultimately, they should be killed. Doesn't that sound vaguely familiar? Every one of these persecutions had a precedent in earlier centuries when the Church controlled politics. Hitler really did not do anything new, he only did it on a grander scale, and more "efficiently." Sadly, he learned his lesson from Church history.

A 1987 Japanese edition of "The Protocols," warning of the imminent threat of a global Jewish takeover.

Hitler and his agents were certainly not true Christians. Nazi philosophy was influenced more by pagan mythology. But most Nazis were members in good standing in either Lutheran or Catholic churches. They perpetrated these acts in a historically Christian nation...and there was a deafening silence from the Christian world. Even during the decade before the Final Solution exterminations began, the "Christian West" rejected Jewish emigrants fleeing from the growing Nazi menace, and even prevented them from going to Eretz Israel, their ancestral homeland. These decisions resulted in the death of millions.

Pastor Neimoeller, writing of this sad chapter of history, said: "First they came for the Communists and I did not speak out - because I was not a Communist. Then they came for the Socialists and I did not speak out - because I was not a Socialist. Then they came for the trade unionists and I did not speak out - because I was not a trade unionist. Then they came for the Jews and I did not speak out - because I was not a Jew. Then they came for me - and there was no one left to speak out for me."

The Holocaust in all of its severity is unique to the Jewish people. While non-Jews were killed in Hitler's killing machine, they were killed for political or social reasons, such as being mentally ill, prostitutes or homosexuals. The Jewish people as a whole were targets: mothers, children, peasants, doctors, musicians, rabbis, professors, etc. None were exempt, and they were all exterminated JUST BECAUSE THEY WERE JEWS. Fortunately, there were some Christians who acted with compassion to hide or help Jews to escape, e.g. Corrie Ten Boom and the Christians of Le Chambon in France. However, their numbers were far too few to make a significant difference.

Hitler is gone. Nazi Germany has ceased to exist. However, the *"apple of God's eye"* (Zech. 2:8), the Jewish people, are alive, and Israel is a fact.

ANTI-SEMITISM IN THE LAST 50 YEARS

From this historical account, it can be seen that the concept of Christian-Jewish relations is a very recent phenomenon. The effort to build genuine Christian-Jewish relationships has only begun in a serious fashion during the last 40 years. Forty years out of nearly 2,000 is not a long time. Much of this effort is in response to the Holocaust; nevertheless, it is happening. Will it last? Only if you are a part of making it last. There is still a battle to be fought. Anti-Semitism isn't gone, and can be seen or heard in every community. While some would have you believe the world is becoming a better place and anti-Semitism is on the wane, this is not true. Since 1990, anti-Semitic acts around the world have increased, even showing up in places where hardly any Jews live, such as Japan.

Dayan to Hitler: Move on!

Political cartoon from "Pravada," the Soviet newspaper. Moshe Dayan is depicted as displacing Hitler from his post as champion tyrant after the Six-Day War in 1967.

We also see how Israel receives a great deal of media reporting that is tainted with a perpetually negative bias. Israel has become a bastion of self-determination for the Jewish people, and many in the world cannot accept it. A "weak underdog" Israel was more acceptable. But a strong Israel, on equal par in the world, is unacceptable.

In my estimation, world opinion of Israel is trapped in the old pit of anti-Semitism. After World War II, as the facts of the Holocaust came to light, many enlightened individuals and groups began to speak out for the Jewish people, albeit too late to save the 6,000,000 who perished. While it was no longer "fashionable" to be anti-Semitic, that did not make the problem go away...it only drove it underground. Currently, it is showing itself in world opinion of Israel, as people and governments have transferred their anti-Semitic feelings to a national or political level in the disguise of righteous indignation against the "aggressive Zionist State." The new anti-Israel, or anti-Zionist trend, is nothing more than the old anti-Semitism in new clothing.

How can we counteract this? We can take a stand, know our facts, and be a collective Christian voice of support and encouragement. This is something that hasn't been done during all Church history. Yes, there have been Christian individuals who spoke out, but now I believe we have a chance to make a difference because we can show solidarity as a group.

WHAT SHOULD THIS MEAN TO US?

The Jewish people know this history well, while most Christians often ignore it. We prefer to forget about it, because it is an indictment against us.

Rev. Dr. Edward Flannery, in his book, *The Anguish of the Jews*, says that "the only chapters of Christian history known by the Jews were recorded on pages the Church has torn out of the history books and burned."

What does Paul mean in Romans 11 when he points out that the Jewish people are *"beloved for the sake of the Fathers,"* and that, *"by our mercy, they will receive mercy?"*

It is grievous to think that one of Satan's greatest tools against God's covenant people, the apple of His eye, has been the Church. To say that these historical churchmen who did these terrible things were not real Christians is not accurate, for many of them were.

Let us learn a lesson from Martin Luther. No one can doubt his devotion to the Lord, yet he wrote and spoke some of the most terrible anti-Semitic material in history. Like Luther, some of the greatest anti-Semites started out as great supporters of the Jewish people, and then became disappointed when Jews did not fulfill Christian expectations. Apparently, their love was not genuine, but had an ulterior motive. Anti-Semitism is sin and we must constantly guard against it in our hearts and lives. I fully believe that anti-Semitism is the epitome of evil, and the fight against it is a spiritual, as well as a physical, battle. Since the Jews are a God-called, covenantal people, to fight against them is to fight against God. This may be understandable for those of the world, but a tragic error for Christians who believe in the God of Israel. As Ogden Nash wrote, "How odd of God to chose the Jews, but not so odd as those who chose the Jewish God and spurn the Jews."

Let us pray this is a new day - when the Church will show love and learn to respect God's covenant people, our elder brothers; and biblical Judaism, the parent faith of our faith.

Isaiah the prophet said, *"Listen to me, you who pursue righteousness and who seek the Lord; Look to the rock from which you were cut and to the quarry from which you were hewn; look to Abraham, your father and to Sarah, who gave you birth. When I called him, he was but one, and I blessed him and made him many. The Lord will surely comfort Zion and will look with compassion on all her ruins..."* (Isa. 51:1-3). Paul says, *"...if the root is holy, so are the branches. If some of the branches have been broken off, and you, though a wild olive shoot, have been grafted in among the others and now share in the nourishing sap from the olive root, do not boast over those branches. If you do, consider this: you do not support the root, but the root supports you"* (Rom. 11:16-18).

Paul is clear about God's natural branches, the Jewish people, when he says of them in Romans 11:28, *"They are beloved for the sakes of the Patriarchs, for God's gifts and His call are irrevocable."*

Bridges for Peace Christian volunteers join a Jewish social worker to provide food and comfort to one of Jerusalem's elderly.

Christians need to remember, it was by the Jewish people, God's Chosen people, that Jesus was born, and by whom we received God's gift of salvation. They were chosen to live in God's land, Israel, to worship God and be blessed by Him, thus showing the world the blessedness of serving the one true God. They were also chosen to receive and record God's Word so we could have the Bible. Yes, they should be loved for what they have given to us, not hated. It has been pointed out that the Jewish people are not perfect and have made mistakes as well. Through their hurt, many have even learned to fear and hate Christians and Christianity. Yet, this is still no excuse for us to act against them, now or in the past.

As Gentile Christians, we have a Jewish connection. In Ephesians 2:11-13, Paul tells us that we Gentiles have been *"brought near"* by the blood of Jesus to the covenants of the promises, hopes and faith of Israel, and even made citizens of Israel.

Further, we must remember that Jesus was Jewish. His actual name was Yeshua, and He was a rabbi who taught in the synagogues. His disciples and the writers of the New Testament, except Luke, were Jewish, and the apostles and early disciples were Jewish. They worshipped on Shabbat (Saturday), celebrated the feasts, and attended Synagogue.

Paul tells Christians, *"that by our mercy they shall receive God's mercy."* This love and mercy towards the Jewish people is more than a warm feeling of appreciation. As Christians, we have a debt to Israel.

In Romans 15:27, Paul says we need to demonstrate our love and mercy with action, when he says, *"For if the Gentiles have shared in the Jews' spiritual blessings, they owe it to the Jews to share with them their material blessings."*

In Matthew 25, Jesus Himself takes a stand on this issue when He equates how we treat His brethren, the Jewish people, with how we treat Him. In verses 34-40, Jesus says He was hungry, thirsty, a stranger, in need of clothes, sick and in prison. He then declared that His disciples attended to all of these needs. They answered, "Lord, when did we see You in these situations?" And, He replied, *"I tell you the truth, whatever you did for one of the least of these My brothers, you did for Me."*

Zechariah 2:8 says of God's love towards the Jewish people, *"He that touches you, touches the apple of His eye."*

Today, we can read the Bible for ourselves, and see God's love for His people, Israel. Therefore:

- It is time for Christians to break with historical anti-Jewish teachings, and make a change for the future. We must act, not out of guilt, but in a humble spirit of love.
- It is time to reinforce God's covenant WITH His people, and show tangible love and respect to the Jewish people around the world.
- It is also time to join God in His plan for the nation of Israel today, as He is literally moving heaven and earth to fulfill His prophetic promises of Messianic blessing, as we await the soon coming of the Lord.

As Christians, let us take up the challenge and put aside the anti-Jewish hatred of generations, wherever it may be found around us — be it in our communities, in our churches, in our families, and yes, even if it rises up in our own hearts.

The destiny of the Church is intertwined with the future of Israel and the Jewish people. For too long, Christians have been silent. For too long, the Jewish community has had to fight its battles alone. It is time for each one of us to speak up for the people who gave us the Bible and our Savior.

Each one of us can make a difference.

This Lesson from the Land of the Bible is found in our
Jerusalem Mosaic Video Series, Program #112,
along with other exciting features.
Please turn to page 186 to order your copy.

Bibliography

Aumann, Moshe, *Land Ownership in Palestine 1880-1948*, Israel Academic Committee on the Middle East, Jerusalem, Israel, 1976.

Brubaker, Gordon, *"Life in Bible Times,"* selected article, 1984.

Church, J. R., *"The Prophecy of Elijah's Mantle,"* Prophecy in the News, 1998.

Davis, Leonard J., *Myths and Facts: A Concise Record of the Arab-Israeli Conflict*, Near East Report, Washington, DC, USA, 1985.

Edersheim, Alfred, *The Life and Times of Jesus, the Messiah*, London, UK, 1890.

The Encyclopedia Judaica, Keter Publishing House, Ltd., Jerusalem, Israel, 1978.

Flannery, Edward H., *The Anguish of the Jews*, Paulist Press, New York, USA, 1985.

Fleming, Dr. James, *"The Last Supper"* in the Jesus Christ Video Series, Tape 5, 1986; *"Biblical Teachings and Mealtime Customs"* in the Scripture Garden Video Series, Tape 1, 1992; *"The Context of Holy Week"* Bible Conference Audio, Video, and Conference Notebook, 1997; audio lecture, *Touching the Fringe of His Garment*, Biblical Resources Study Center, Jerusalem, Israel.*

Gerrish, Jim, *Jerusalem Prayer Letter*, Jerusalem, Israel.

Gospel Parallels: A Synopsis of the First Three Gospels, Thomas Nelson Publishers, New York, USA, 1979.

Granott, A., *The Land System in Palestine*, London, 1952.

The Holy Bible, New International Version, Zondervan Bible Publishers, Grand Rapids, MI, USA, 1978.

The Holy Bible, King James Version, Oxford University Press, New York, USA, 1967.

Josephus, Flavius, *The Wars of the Jews*, Baker Book House, Grand Rapids, MI, USA, 1974.

Lambert, Lance, *The Uniqueness of Israel,* Kingsway Publications, Eastbourne, E. Sussex, UK, 1980.

Monson, James, *Historical Geography of the Bible Lands,* Pictorial Archive (Near East History), Jerusalem, Israel, 1979.

Pamphilus, Eusebius, *The Ecclesiastical History,* Baker Book House, Grand Rapids, MI, USA, 1991.

Rausch, David A., *A Legacy of Hatred,* Moody Press, Chicago, IL, USA, 1984.

Strong, James, *Strong's Exhaustive Concordance of the Bible,* Thomas Nelson Publishers, Nashville, TN, USA, 1979.

Twain, Mark, *The Innocents Abroad,* The American Publishing Company, Hartford, CT, USA, 1869.

Wilson, William, *Wilson's Old Testament Word Studies,* Hendrickson Publishers, Peabody, MA, USA.

Young, G. Douglas, *Young's Compact Bible Dictionary,* Tyndale House Publishers, Wheaton, IL, USA, 1984.

The Zondervan Pictorial Encyclopedia of the Bible (5 volumes), Zondervan Bible Publishers, Grand Rapids, MI, USA, 1976.

Vine, W.E., *Vine's Expository Dictionary of Old and New Testament Words,* Fleming H. Revell, Grand Rapids, MI, USA, 1981.

Wagner, Jr., Clarence H., *"Everyday Life in Bible Times," Almanac of the Bible,* Prentice Hall, New York, USA, 1991.

*For information on resources offered by Biblical Resources Study Center, write to: P.O. Box 1970, Bellaire, TX 77402, USA.

ResourceS

Why just read
about Bible Prophecy
when you
can be a part of it?

BRIDGES FOR PEACE – is a Jerusalem-based, multi-faceted, Christian organization dedicated to the building of sincere relationships between the Christian and Jewish communities, while encouraging greater concern for the land and people of Israel. It is our desire to see Christians and Jews working side by side for better understanding and a more secure Israel.

Founded in 1976, Bridges for Peace seeks to be a ministry of hope and reconciliation. Through programs both in Israel and worldwide, we are giving Christians the opportunity to actively express their biblical responsibility before God to be faithful to Israel and the Jewish community.

For too long Christians have been silent. For too long the Jewish community has had to fight its battles alone. It is time Christian individuals and congregations speak up for the people who gave us the Bible.

We are committed to the following goals:
❖ Interpreting Israel to Christians in light of the Bible and today's events.
❖ Providing counsel and channels of service for pro-Israel groups and individuals desiring to actively support and bless Israel and the Jewish people.
❖ Working to combat anti-Semitism and all forms of prejudice and misunderstanding between Christians and Jews.
❖ Bringing Christian concerns to the attention of appropriate Israeli leaders and to the Jewish community at large.
❖ Developing and providing a variety of study materials and aids to churches, schools, and tour groups to prepare Christians for an in-depth understanding of Israel and the Jewish roots of our Christian faith.

We are accomplishing this through a variety of programs:
❖ *Dispatch from Jerusalem:* A bi-monthly publication with pertinent and positive news from Israel, and informative insights into the hopes and aspirations of the Israeli people, all in a prophetic context.
❖ *Israel Teaching Letter:* Monthly in-depth studies bringing to light the fuller meanings of biblical concepts from the Hebraic roots of the Scriptures.
❖ *Jerusalem Mosaic:* A weekly television series, shot on location in Israel, which brings the Land of the Bible and her people direct from Israel to you.
❖ *Israel Current News & Prayer Update:* Weekly e-mail update. To subscribe, send the message: subscribe bfp-update <your name> from your e-mail address, to Update, at listproc@grmi.org

❖ **Galilee Study Center:** Overlooking the Sea of Galilee, our center offers a directed study program, spacious accomodations, and a 2,000 book library. It is a welcome retreat for those who wish to relax or study.

❖ **Chai Night Prayer and Study Groups:** A monthly intercessory prayer program sponsored by individuals and churches around the world who desire to *"Pray for the Peace of Jerusalem."*

❖ **Bridge-Building Projects:** Promote better Christian-Jewish understanding and support for Israel on the local and regional level around the world. Projects such as Hebrew classes, film series, Israel Awareness Programs, speakers bureau, study seminars, etc. are offered.

❖ **Operation Ezra:** A vital social assistance program providing a channel of practical help to a variety of worthy projects in Israel utilizing cash contributions and gifts-in-kind from Christians to bless Israel. Through our Food Bank, food gifts are channelled to help Israel's needy (both Jews and Arabs). Currently we are assisting Jewish immigrants to Israel, Israel's elderly and poor, and Arab believers.

❖ **Project Rescue/Project Hope:** These programs help the poorest Jews, from the countries of the former Soviet Union, prepare to immigrate to Israel, (Project Rescue) and helps sustain those who cannot come, the elderly and the sick (Project Hope). Without our help most would find the cost of passports, visas, ground transportation, lodging, etc. out of their reach.

❖ **Short Term Service:** A wonderful opportunity for Christians to build sincere relationships by volunteering to serve as short term staff assisting Israel's poor and new immigrants directly via our BFP Food Bank/Distribution Center, Gleaning Program, and Home Repair Project.

❖ **Bridges for Peace Forest in Israel:** Located on Mt. Tabor, this forest gives Christians the opportunity to participate in the greening of Israel and the fulfillment of the prophecies about the restoration of the Land.

❖ **Bible Study Tours in Israel:** Bridges for Peace provides a variety of travel opportunities and lectures to help you or your tour group gain a deeper understanding of Israel, the Jewish people and the Jewish roots of our Christian faith in light of the Bible, history, archaeology, and current events. An extensive pre-travel study manual is a part of all BFP tours, and is also available to individuals or tour groups coming to Israel.

FOR MORE INFORMATION, write to any of our national offices. We are also available to help you plan activities in your area. When you come to Israel we would like to meet you or speak for your group. Please contact us in advance, or visit our International Headquarters located at 7 Shaul Adler, Jerusalem, Israel. Phone: 972-2-624-5004, FAX: 972-2-624-6622

We invite you to join us in a practical expression of this desire to bless Israel by becoming an active Bridge-builder and participating in fulfilling biblical prophecy through the vital and important work of Bridges for Peace. (See coupon on page 186).

Operation Ezra

Bridges for Peace, an evangelical Christian organization, has joined God's prophetic plan to rebuild Zion. Inspired by the book of Ezra, we tangibly help the Jewish people, God's covenant people who are returning to Israel, the land of their forefathers, the land of the Bible, in preparation for the coming of the Messiah!

We give direct aid, illustrated by the following gift items, along with God's love and hope to young and old, the new immigrant and the veteran Israeli. We seek to be your connection to Israel and her people, serving as your hands and feet to personally deliver these gifts. Select your gift(s) today and become a part of Bible prophecy!
(Please see order page)

One in six Israelis live under the poverty line; 436,000 of them are children.

Welcome Kitchen Basket

"I was a stranger and you invited Me in. . ." Matthew 25:35. To help the new immigrants get a start in Israel, our much sought after Welcome Kitchen Basket provides pots, pans, utensils, staple foods and other needed items for the kitchen.

Contribution:
$45 US per basket

A Warm Blanket

"If one of you says to him, 'Go, I wish you well: keep warm and well fed,' but does nothing about his physical needs, what good is it?" James 2:16. Share the warmth of your love! Israel's apartments are built with solid concrete walls, stone floor tiles and are inadequately heated. In winter months, with occasional snow and temperatures around freezing, houses are often like refrigerators. New immigrants and veteran Israelis alike need the blessing of a warm blanket.

Contribution:
$15 US per blanket.

174

Emergency Food Parcel

The Bridges for Peace Food Bank is the first and the largest in Israel. Daily, almost two tons of food passes through the BFP Distribution Center, headed for the homes of Israel's needy. New immigrants benefit as well as those who have been here for a longer time. Holocaust survivors, needy children both in the Jewish and Arab sectors, orphanages, and Jewish community centers are all on our list of recipients. Christian volunteers from all over the world come to help Bridges for Peace welcome new immigrants and help the poor in Israel. Glowing reports keep coming to us, both from recipients and volunteers, about how the center is meeting needs. We will turn your contribution into much needed food.

Contribution: $15 US per parcel

School Starter Kits

"And whoever welcomes a little child like this in My name, welcomes Me."   Matthew 18:5

Let's not forget the immigrant children who arrive with great anticipation of going to school, yet have no supplies. This attractive School Kit contains many of the needed items, including pens, pencils, sharpener, glue, scissors, markers, a carrying case and more.

Contribution : $5 US per school kit

Send out the Gleaners

Like Ruth of old, Bridges for Peace volunteers visit Israeli farms and food processors to glean unused products for the poor and new immigrants. BFP has collected tons of FREE food and other products from the fields and factories of Israel. Your gifts will keep our trucks fueled up and on the road collecting food.

Contribution: $5 US or more

Become A Part Of Bible Prophecy

"For if the Gentiles have shared in the Jews' spiritual blessings, they owe it to the Jews to share with them their material blessings." Romans 15:27

Nearly 1,000,000 new immigrants have come to Israel since 1989.

Many of them live below the poverty line.

Bibles (Dual Translation)

"The grass withers and the flowers fall, but the Word of our God stands forever" Isaiah 40:8.

For many years, Bridges for Peace has provided "food for the body." Now, we are able to provide "food for the soul!" Most new immigrants coming into Israel today arrive from former communist lands where reading the Bible was forbidden. Many have never read a Bible in their lives. How can they come home to Israel in fulfillment of God's Word and not know what the Bible says about it? With your gift, they can read the Word themselves in a Russian-Hebrew translation of the Hebrew Scriptures. Many will be reading it for the first time. They can also learn more Hebrew while learning of God's love for them. Many native Israeli families have never opened the Word of God by themselves. Your gift will put a Hebrew Bible in the hands of struggling Israeli families to offer them solutions in their time of crisis like no other gift can do. (This project is being co-sponsored by the ADL.)

Contribution: $25 US Bible set (3 volumes)

Cheer Basket

"He has sent Me to bind up the brokenhearted" Isaiah 61:1.

Our Cheer Basket is filled with delicious cookies, candies, dried fruit, nuts, flavored teas, and several other items which are specifically selected to bring hope and encouragement to Israel's shut-ins, the elderly and anyone who is discouraged and needs a tangible expression of God's love.

Contribution: $15 US

The Adoption Program

"Whatever you did for one of the least of these brothers of Mine, you did for Me." Matthew 25:40

The BFP Adoption Program gives you an opportunity to sponsor some of the most needy people in Israel - some of God's covenant people who will "make it" with your helping hand. These include new immigrants who arrive with extreme needs not covered by the small government subsidy for immigrants. Some contemplate leaving Israel, for without a job and language skills, they get discouraged. Their first year is very hard, and many have told us that because of our sponsorship, which provides generous material and emotional support, they were encouraged and succeeded in making a new home in Israel. Through our Israeli Food Program, we have met many veteran Israeli families who are victims of circumstances that threaten to destroy the family, e.g. victims of terror attacks, loss of a breadwinner through death or disability, major medical crises, Holocaust survivors who can't make it alone, etc.

Two Choices of Sponsorship

You may choose to help a NEW IMMIGRANT during their first year of adjustment. Or, you may decide to support an ISRAELI FAMILY in their time of crisis. These Israeli families are part of the nearly 700,000 people in Israel who live below the poverty line. Your assistance helps them lead a more normal life.

What Can You Do?

Your one-year commitment to send monthly assistance, combined with several other sponsors, will provide:

- ❀ Generous food parcels from the BFP Food Bank
- ❀ An unlimited-ride bus pass for the primary job seeker
- ❀ Urgently needed assistance which may include clothing, shoes, diapers, medical or dental aid, etc.
- ❀ Much needed hope and encouragement given by our staff and your letters which money can't buy.

Upon our receipt of your first gift, you will be sent the name and profile of your adoptees, including a photograph (if available). We encourage the exchange of letters between you and your adoptees, and we will assist in translation. Since this information is coming from Jerusalem, please allow 6-8 weeks for delivery.

Contribution: - $30 US/mo. for an individual
Contribution: - $50 US/mo. for a family
  Choose a New immigrant or Israeli family.

Participate in Bible Prophecy!
Operation Ezra

Project Rescue

"The days are coming," declares the Lord, "when men will no longer say, 'As surely as the Lord lives, who brought the Israelites up out of Egypt,' but they will say, 'As surely as the Lord lives, who brought the Israelites up out of the land of the north and out of all the countries where He had banished them.' For I will restore them to the land I gave their forefathers. But, now I will send for many fishermen," declares the Lord, *"and they will catch them"* Jeremiah 16:14-16.

We discovered that many of the neediest Jews from the countries of the former Soviet Union were unable to come to Israel because they simply could not afford the cost of passports, exit visas, ground transportation, lodging, etc. for their trip home. We send "fishermen" who search for hopeless Russian Jews who still long to go "Home." Without our help, they would be unable to immigrate to Israel. With your help, we can literally "rescue" our Jewish brothers and help them fulfill God's Word.

$300 US to rescue one person (Any portion of that cost will apply toward one person.)

Repairers of the Breach

In Isaiah 58:12, the prophet calls those who help rebuild Zion, *"repairers of the breach and restorers of the streets with dwellings."* God has blessed Bridges for Peace with skilled construction workers. Teams are busy ren-

ovating homes of the poor and elderly, many of whom are Holocaust survivors. Many of these homes are one-room hovels in buildings over 100 years old. We fix leaky plumbing, replace broken windows, paint, plaster, rewire, repair or install cabinets, put on new roofs, and do general fix-up work. Some of our workers have told us that this is the best job they have ever had in their lives. They get many hugs, plus a lot of tea, coffee and cake from very appreciative Jerusalemites. Your gifts supply the raw materials to get the job done.

Contribution:
$10 US or more

Do-It-Yourself Project

In the Bible, Ezra not only used offerings of money to rebuild Zion, but also tangible gifts. You can be like Ezra. Many Christian pilgrims come to the land of Israel at some time in their life. Maybe you will come, or someone you know. When you do, you can bring important items for distribution in our Operation Ezra Programs. Simply purchase these items yourself (or with help from your church or prayer group) and pack them into your suitcase (or an extra suitcase which can accompany you free of charge when coming from North America). There is no customs duty on these items when brought by a tourist.

What is needed?

- New items for newborns
- New children's clothing of all kinds
- New underwear, shoes, socks, and sweaters (all sizes)
- School supplies for the children
- New toys (non-verbal)
- Small kitchen utensils and gadgets of all kinds
- Pot holders and oven mitts
- New kitchen and bathroom towels
- Bedsheets, flat (not fitted)
- Yarn and embroidery floss (bright colors) for Ethiopian handicrafts and blind women who have learned to knit and weave
- New medical supplies, e.g. surgical tape, gauze, bandages, band-aides and vitamins (especially pre-natal, infant drops with iron, and children's chewable vitamins)
- Toothpaste, toothbrushes, soap, deodorant and shampoo
- Baby formula (powdered)

Thanks from Those We Help

- *"I wait for Wednesday when you deliver food. It is my favorite day."*
  - from Rachel Yoni, an elderly recipient of food

- *"I don't understand why you Christians help us Jews. You have been our enemies for many generations. I cannot tell you how much your help has kept us alive in Israel. I know God is looking after me and my family. Thank you for helping us."*
  - from a father on the BFP Adoption Program, with tears rolling down his cheeks

- *"The supplies we receive from Bridges For Peace help us to help those suffering from Chernobyl-induced cancer. They have limited resources and many needs. In Russia, I was a communist. Here in Israel, I have come to believe in God. I am happy I can help others."*
  - Gregory Filkovsky, founder of Love to Life organization, which receives food from BFP

Donation amounts are quoted in US dollars for reference. Contributions can be made in equivalent local currency and sent to your nearest national office. Please see the order page. Addresses also included in resources section. Thank you for caring and sharing.

365 Fascinating Facts about the Holy Land

by Clarence H. Wagner Jr.
Brings the land of Israel to life.

Packed with a wealth of information about "Eretz Israel," the Land of Israel, *365 Fascinating Facts About The Holy Land*, by Clarence H. Wagner, Jr., is one of the most important handbooks on this magnificent land on the market.

Concise information covers a broad range of topics from: culture, customs, and climate, to Middle East politics, wars, and efforts for peace.

Add to your knowledge with such facts as:

- "Palestine" was a word coined by the Roman Empire after the time of Christ.
- Israel today is a leading exporter of flowers, fulfilling the prophecies of Ezekiel.
- Modern Israel, just over 50 years old, is barely younger than the neighboring states of Jordan, Syria, and Iraq.

To order your book please contact: Bridges for Peace, $10.95 + 10% s/h or use order form in the back of this book.

Sounds of Zion

Jerusalem Mosaic's music video,

12 moving songs by Christian artists, as seen on the Jerusalem Mosaic television series. Filmed on location in Israel, you will rejoice with those who bring God's message in music from Jerusalem, the city of the Great King. May the praises of God fill your heart as you join us in praising the Lord in Zion.

The Promised Land
Tommy Williams
Tourmaline Music, Inc.

The Lord Has Chosen Zion
Chuck King
Sharewater Music/BMI

I Will Bless
Mike & Melissa Mott
Cynthia Conner

Those Who Trust in the Lord
Chuck King
Sharewater Music/BMI

Od Ye Shama
Roy Kendall
Public Domain

May the Lord Bless You Out of Zion
Chuck King
Sharewater Music/BMI

Eretz Israel
Tommy Williams
Tourmaline Music, Inc.

Pray for the Peace of Jerusalem
Chuck King
Sharewater Music/BMI

I Will Listen
Mike & Melissa Mott
EMI Christian Music Publishing

Those Who Sow in Tears
Chuck King
Sharewater Music/BMI

Shalom (My Friend)
Tommy Williams
Tourmaline Music, Inc.

O Lord God of Israel
Carol Cantrell
Integrity's Hosanna!
Music/ASCAP

Now available for only US$19.95 each.
Shipping and handling: 10%. Credit card orders accepted.

To order use coupon on page 186.

Filmed on location in Israel
Jerusalem Mosaic
brings to you:

- New insights into the words of Jesus
- Current fulfillment of Bible prophecy
- News behind the news
- Faces of Israeli life, culture and history
- Breathtaking scenery of the Land of the Bible
- Beautiful inspirational music sung by Christian artists
  Take the journey of a lifetime without leaving your home,
  and see God's Word come alive!

Now, the popular television 13-part series is available for home viewing!

- Share your love of God and Israel with family,
  friends and prayer groups
- Teach your children and grandchildren about
  God's living Word
- A great resource for Home Schoolers and Sunday
  school teachers
- Give *Jerusalem Mosaic* as a gift to your pastor,
  friend or church/school library
- View *Jerusalem Mosaic* over and over again, to enrich
  your understanding of the Bible

SPECIAL OFFER: The entire 13-part series for the price of 10 at only US $149.95 + 10% shipping and handling - A savings of 23% over the single price! Credit card orders accepted in the US and Canada. Individual videos available for only US $14.95 each plus 10% shipping and handling.

✡ **101 - Teaching: "Hem of the Garment"**
- Bar Mitzvah at the Western Wall - Archaeology: Under the Seibenberg House - Biblical Artist Pam Suran - Song: "Those Who Sow in Tears"

✡ **102 - Teaching: "Passover-Last Supper Connection"**
- Life on a Kibbutz - Immigrant Art Program
- Interview with Derek Prince - Song: "Those Who Trust in the Lord"

✡ **103 - Teaching: "The Return to Zion"**
- Life on the Golan Heights - Biblical Harp Making
- Rescuing Jewish Immigrants - Song: "The Promised Land"

✡ **104 - Teaching: "Life in Bible Times"**
- Archaeology: Hatzor and Joshua's Conquest
- Restoring Ancient Artifacts - Armenian Pottery
- Song: "May the Lord Bless You Out Of Zion"

✡ **105 - Teaching: "The Flowers of Israel"**
- Growing Flowers in the Desert - Cartoonist Ya'acov Kirschen
- BFP/Christian Volunteering in Israel - Song: "Eretz Israel"

✡ **106 - Teaching: "What's in a Name?"**
- Dead Sea Scrolls, 50 Years Later - Scribes Continue their Ancient Craft
- An Ethiopian's Story - Song: "I Will Bless"

✡ **107 - Teaching: "The Trumpet is Sounding in Zion"**
- Jerusalem Day - Interview with Mayor Ehud Olmert - Jerusalem's Outdoor Produce Market - Song: "Pray for the Peace of Jerusalem"

✡ **108 - Teaching: "The Covenant Meal"**
- Biblical Fishing Methods - Ancient Olive Pressing
- How the Bible is Being Taught in Israeli Schools
- Song: "I Will Listen"

✡ **109 - Teaching: "The Land in Between/Geography of the Bible"**
- The Miracle of Eilat - The Greening of Israel
- Camel Trekking - Song: "Od Ye Shama"

✡ **110 - Teaching: "The Threshing Floor"**
- Matza Making Excitement - Israeli Agri-Tech: Microscopic Worms Used as Pesticides - Food For Needy Israelis
- Song: "The Lord Has Chosen Zion"

✡ **111 - Teaching: "Sukkot - Feast of Tabernacles"**
- Feast of Tabernacles in Jerusalem - Hasmonean Tunnels
- Repairing the Walls of Zion - Song: "Shalom My Friend"

✡ **112 - Teaching: "The Legacy of Hatred:**
  Anti-Semitism in the Church"
- Righteous Gentiles Who Rescued Jews in WWII
- Interview and Music by Adrian Snell

✡ **113 - Teaching: "Guarding Your Gates"**
- Artistic Creations with Roman Glass
- BFP Adopt-an-Immigrant Story
- Song: "O Lord God of Israel"

BFP Publications

FREE
Six-Month
Subscription

- *Dispatch from Jerusalem* - a 20 page bi-monthly newspaper with pertinent and positive news from Israel in a prophetic context.

- *Israel Teaching Letter* - Monthly in-depth studies exploring the fuller meanings of biblical concepts from the Hebraic roots of the Scriptures.

- *Israel Current News and Prayer Update* - Weekly Email News Update with prayer focus from Israel. To subscribe, send the message: subscribe bfp-update<your name> from your e-mail address, to Update, at listproc@grmi.org

- *Comprehensive Web Site* - www.bridgesforpeace.com

Write Today!!
Use Coupon on page 186

 *Please send me:*

❑ **Jerusalem Mosaic** videos - Please mark the box to the left of desired videos. If ordering more than one copy, place quantity being ordered on line following number.

❑ **Special Offer:** 13 Video Series ____ (US$ 149.95 + 10% s/h* *or* US$ 14.95 each + s/h*)

❑ #101___ ❑ #102___ ❑ #103___ ❑ #104___ ❑ #105___
❑ #106___ ❑ #107 ___ ❑ #108___ ❑ #109___ ❑ #110___
❑ #111___ ❑ #112___ ❑ #113___

❑ **Sounds of Zion** video(s) - Please send me _____ . Now available for only US$19.95 each + s/h*.

❑ **365 Facinating Facts about the Holy land** by Clarence H. Wagner, Jr.
- Please send me_____ US$10.99 + s/h*

❑ **Free subscription** to the *Dispatch from Jerusalem* and *Israel Teaching Letter*.

❑ **Free subscription** to *Israel Current News & Prayer Update* - weekly email service.

❑ **Ezra Projects** - Please use my gift of $_____ for the following: (Indicate quantity of each gift on line preceding gift number.)

*Shipping and handling: 10%

____ Gift #1 -- US$45 Kitchen Basket
____ Gift #2 -- US$15 Blanket
____ Gift #3 -- US$15 Food Parcel
____ Gift #4 -- US$ 5 School Kit
____ Gift #5 -- US$ 5 or more per Gleaner

____ Gift # 6 -- US$30 Adopted Individual
____ Gift # 7 -- US$50 Adopted Family
____ Gift # 8 -- US$15 Cheer Gift
____ Gift # 9 -- US$25 Bible Set (3 Vol)
____ Gift #10 -- US$10 or more Repair Crew
____ Gift #11 -- US$300 Project Rescue

Ezra Projects _____		US$_____
Number of single videos ordered _____	@US$14.95	$_____
Entire 13-part series Special Offer _____	@US$149.95	$_____
Sound of Zion Videos ordered _____	@ US$19.95	$_____
365 Fascinating Facts book ordered _____	@US$10.99	$_____
Shipping and handling 10%		$_____
Total		US$_____

Name:_____

Address:_____

City: _____ State/Prov: _____

Code: _____ Tel: _____

E-Mail: _____ (Please print clearly.)

Make checks payable to Bridges for Peace or charge my:

❑ Visa ❑ MasterCard ❑ Discover (International cards only)

Card No.: _____ Exp. Date: _____

Signature: _____

Clip and send coupon to Bridges for Peace, P.O. Box 1093, Jerusalem, Israel
Phone orders accepted in USA and Canada: 1-800-566-1998
(see page 187 for addresses of National offices)

BRIDGES FOR PEACE
NATIONAL OFFICES

INTERNATIONAL HEADQUARTERS: P.O. Box 1093, Jerusalem, Israel
Tel: 972-2-624-5004, FAX: 972-2-624-6622

U.S.: P.O. Box 33145, Tulsa OK 74153-1145 Tel: (918) 461-8800,
FAX: (918) 461-8808

CANADA: P.O. Box 21001, RPO Charleswood, Winnipeg, MB
R3R 3R2 Tel: (204) 489-3697, FAX: (204) 489-7998

U.K.: Victoria House, Victoria Road, Buckhurst Hill, Essex IG9 5EX
Tel: (44) 208-559-2479, FAX: (44) 208-502-9062

SOUTH AFRICA: P.O. Box 15263, Panorama, 7506, RSA
Tel/FAX: (27) 21-975-1941

JAPAN: 2-1 OCC 5F Kandasurugadai, Chiyoda-ku, Tokyo 101-0062
Tel: (81) 3-5283-7333, FAX: (81) 3-5283-7337

BRAZIL: Caixa Postal:1197, Cep: 30.123-970 BH - MG
Tel: 55-31-378-9350

PUERTO RICO: PMB 133, 100 Ave. Grand Blvd. Suite 112,
San Juan, PR 00926-5955 EUA Tel/FAX: (787) 782-0868

AUSTRALIA: P.O. Box 7973, GCMC, Queensland 9726
Tel: 0061-7-5570-6161, FAX: 0061-7-5561-0835